Better Homes and Gardens®
salads & appetizers

AMERICA'S BEST-LOVED COMMUNITY COOKBOOK RECIPES

BETTER HOMES AND GARDENS® BOOKS
DES MOINES

BETTER HOMES AND GARDENS® BOOKS
An Imprint of Meredith® Books

America's Best-Loved Community Cookbook Recipes
Salads and Appetizers
Editor: Christopher Cavanaugh
Copy Chief: Gregory H. Kayko
Associate Art Director: Tom Wegner
Designers: Terry Kopel, Jeff Harrison
Copywriter: Kim Gayton Elliott
Production Manager: Bill Rose

Director, New Product Development: Ray Wolf
Test Kitchen Director: Sharon Stilwell

Meredith Publishing Group
President, Publishing Group: Christopher Little
Vice President and Publishing Director: John P. Loughlin

Meredith Corporation
Chairman and Chief Executive Officer: Jack D. Rehm
President and Chief Operating Officer: William T. Kerr

Chairman of the Executive Committee: E.T. Meredith III

Our seal assures you that every recipe in **America's Best-Loved Community Cookbook Recipes: Salads and Appetizers** has been tested in the Better Homes and Gardens® Test Kitchen. This means that each recipe is practical and reliable, and meets our high standards of taste appeal. We guarantee your satisfaction with this book for as long as you own it.

salads & appetizers

Across America—from Oregon to Delaware, North Dakota to New Mexico—people are rediscovering the joy of home cooking. And the great pleasure of sharing collections of these recipes with friends and neighbors while helping the communities in which they live. Schools, hospitals, libraries, and museums have all benefited from community cookbooks—as have the delighted cooks inspired by these remarkable recipes. Now *Better Homes and Gardens®* has selected the very best recipes from these heartfelt community cookbooks and is very pleased to make this wealth of wonderful recipes available to you.

In *Salads and Appetizers,* you'll find an amazing array of mouth-watering appetizers, soups, and salads, from elegant Chilled Shrimp with Herbed Cheese Filling to soul-warming Autumn Bisque to colorful Confetti Rice Salad. Plus, each and every recipe in this book has passed the *Better Homes and Gardens® Test Kitchen* and earned the *Better Homes and Gardens® Test Kitchen Seal of Approval*—so you're guaranteed success any time you make one of these delectable dishes. And our Test Kitchens have added time-saving tips, serving suggestions, and nuggets of professional know-how to help make your cooking experience smooth and easy.

Dishes steeped in tradition, new variations on family favorites, and innovative uses of familiar ingredients—you'll find all that and more in *America's Best-Loved Community Cookbook Recipes: Salads and Appetizers.* With one taste, you'll know that communities across America are really cooking!

contents

cold
hors d'oeuvres

Traditional Cucumber Sandwiches stand side-by-side with exotic Shrimp Balls in this choice assembly of cold appetizers. Any gathering, large or small, would benefit from these tasty tidbits—many of which can be prepared ahead of time for easy entertaining. For a casual get-together, offer Cheddar Crisps or Six-Layer Party Dip. When elegance is the mode, Salmon Hors d'oeuvres will serve the company with distinction. And for feeding a crowd, nothing beats the World's Best Deviled Eggs. With these hors d'oeuvres, you can start any social event with style.

CHEDDAR CRISPS

CHEDDAR CRISPS

Makes 32 Crackers
1¾ cups all-purpose flour
½ cup yellow cornmeal
½ teaspoon baking soda
½ teaspoon sugar
½ teaspoon salt
½ cup butter *or* margarine
1½ cups shredded extra sharp
cheddar cheese (6 ounces)
½ cup cold water
2 tablespoons white vinegar
Coarsely ground black pepper

♦   ♦   ♦

The Ladies Aid of St. John's Lutheran Church has compiled Cooking with a Country Flair in order to raise funds for an addition to their church. The cookbook features over 700 excellent recipes, including Lucy King's Cheddar Crisps. Lucy told us that she likes to make these crackers to serve with soup or to munch as a snack.

Lucy King
Cooking with a Country Flair
St. John's Lutheran Church
Amlin
OHIO

1 Preheat the oven to 375°. Grease a large baking sheet. Set aside.

2 In a large mixing bowl, stir together the flour, cornmeal, baking soda, sugar and salt. Using a pastry blender, cut in the butter or margarine until the mixture resembles coarse crumbs.

3 Using a fork, stir in the shredded cheese, cold water and vinegar just until the mixture forms a soft dough. If necessary, knead the mixture in the bowl until smooth. Shape the dough into a ball. Wrap the ball with plastic wrap and refrigerate about 1 hour or until it is firm enough to handle.

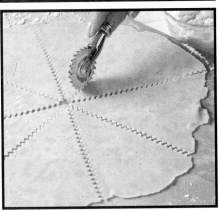

4 On a lightly floured surface, use a floured rolling pin to roll *one-fourth* of the dough into a paper-thin round approximately 13 inches in diameter (edges may be ragged). Keep the remaining dough refrigerated. Using a fluted pastry cutter or a pizza cutter, cut the round into 8 wedges.

5 Transfer the wedges to the prepared baking sheet. Sprinkle the crackers with the black pepper. Firmly press the pepper into the dough. Bake in the 375° oven for 8 to 10 minutes or until browned and crisp. Transfer the crackers to wire racks to cool. Repeat with the remaining dough. Store the cooled crackers in a tightly covered container.

 TIPS FROM OUR KITCHEN

For variety, sprinkle the crackers with sesame seed or poppy seed instead of pepper. Or, substitute pepper cheese for all or part of the cheddar cheese.

The crackers can be stored in the refrigerator or freezer, although they will lose some of their crispness.

For smaller wedges, divide the dough into 8 equal portions. Roll *one-eighth* of the dough into a paper-thin round, approximately 10 inches in diameter. Cut into 8 wedges. This will yield 64 crackers.

Nutrition Analysis (*Per Cracker*): Calories: 78 / Cholesterol: 13 mg / Carbohydrates: 7 g / Protein: 2 g / Sodium: 117 mg / Fat: 5 g (Saturated Fat: 3 g) / Potassium: 17 mg.

PARMESAN TWISTS

Makes 48 Twists

- ½ cup grated Parmesan cheese
- ¼ cup butter *or* margarine, softened
- ½ cup dairy sour cream
- 1 cup all-purpose flour
- ¼ teaspoon dried thyme, crushed
- ¼ teaspoon dried oregano, crushed
- ⅛ teaspoon dried basil, crushed
- 1 egg yolk, beaten with 1 tablespoon water
- 1 tablespoon sesame *or* poppy seed

◆   ◆   ◆

When Anne Bruno of Madison, Wisconsin created these twists, she never expected they'd be such a hit. Anne remembers being nervous, thinking her invention might be a failure. But, to her delight, Anne says, "The reaction was very, very good." Not only did her friends and family like these tasty treats, they have continued to request them year after year. Truly a culinary success story!

Anne Bruno
<u>*Be Our Guest*</u>
Madison
WISCONSIN

1 Preheat oven to 350°. Grease 2 baking sheets.

2 In a medium bowl, beat together the Parmesan cheese and the butter with an electric mixer until the mixture is fluffy. Beat in the sour cream.

3 In a small bowl, combine the flour with the thyme, oregano and basil. Beat the flour mixture into the cheese mixture. Knead the dough lightly and divide it in half.

4 On a lightly floured surface, roll out the dough into two 12 x 6-inch rectangles. Cut each rectangle into twenty-four 6 x ½-inch strips.

5 Before separating the strips, brush them with the egg yolk-water mixture and sprinkle them with the sesame seed or poppy seed.

6 Holding each strip by the ends, gently twist the pastry 2 or 3 times and place on the prepared baking sheets.

7 Bake the twists in the 350° oven for 10 to 12 minutes or until golden. Remove the twists and cool on wire racks.

 TIPS FROM OUR KITCHEN

In a hurry? Cut the dough into 1-inch squares instead of strips to avoid the time and work of twisting the strips.

Nutrition Analysis *(Per Twist)*: Calories: 29 / Cholesterol: 9 mg / Carbohydrates: 2 g / Protein: 1 g / Sodium: 31 mg / Fat: 2 g (Saturated Fat: 1 g) / Potassium: 9 mg.

PARMESAN TWISTS

PARTY ALMONDS

PARTY ALMONDS

Makes 2 Cups

2 cups whole blanched almonds
3 tablespoons butter *or* margarine
1 teaspoon celery salt
½ teaspoon chili powder
⅛ teaspoon ground red pepper

♦ ♦ ♦

Talk about tried-and-true—Marlene Carl has been making and serving her Party Almonds for 20 years! As a volunteer at the Memorial Hospital in St. Louis, Missouri, Marlene decided to pass on her recipe to the Hospital Auxiliary to include in their fund-raising cookbook, Pier Pleasures. The cookbook became one of the best-selling items in the hospital gift shop. Marlene suggests serving the nuts in a white bowl (she prefers a milk glass bowl) for color contrast.

Marlene Carl
Pier Pleasures
St. Joseph
MISSOURI

1 In a large skillet over medium heat, slowly sauté the almonds in the butter or margarine about 6 minutes or until the almonds are golden. Drain off the excess butter or margarine.

2 In a medium bowl, combine the celery salt with the chili powder and ground red pepper. Toss the almonds with the spice mixture until they are well coated.

3 Spread the almonds on foil to cool. Store in an airtight container.

TIPS FROM OUR KITCHEN

We think this spice mixture tastes great with a variety of nuts. Next time, try the recipe using peanuts, pecans, walnuts or cashews instead of almonds.

These almonds make a great gift. Package them in a festive box or bag and tie it with a ribbon.

For longer storage, place the cooled nuts in a freezer container and freeze up to two months.

For spicy party nuts, choose a hot-style chili powder.

Here is a microwave method for Party Almonds. In a 1½-quart microwave-safe casserole, combine the butter, celery salt, chili powder and red pepper. Cook, uncovered, on 100% power (high) for 40 to 50 seconds or until the butter is melted. Stir in the nuts. Cook, uncovered, for 6 to 7 minutes or until the nuts are toasted, stirring every 2 minutes for the first 4 minutes, then every 30 seconds. Spread the almonds on foil to cool.

Nutrition Analysis *(Per 1/4 Cup)*: Calories: 196 / Cholesterol: 8 mg / Carbohydrates: 6 g / Protein: 6 g / Sodium: 232 mg / Fat: 18 g (Saturated Fat: 3 g) / Potassium: 218 mg.

CUCUMBER SANDWICHES

Makes 10 to 20 Sandwiches
- ½   cup water
- ⅓   cup cider vinegar
- ½   teaspoon salt
- 1   small cucumber, peeled and sliced
- 10 slices day-old white bread *or* firm-textured bread
- 2   tablespoons butter *or* margarine, softened
- 4   ounces cream cheese, softened
- 2   tablespoons mayonnaise *or* salad dressing
- ½   teaspoon Worcestershire sauce
- ⅛   teaspoon pepper
- ⅛   teaspoon garlic salt

♦   ♦   ♦

Critics' Choice Chairperson Mrs. Carl Norwood says that she has been eating Mrs. Everett Meeks's Cucumber Sandwiches ever since she can remember. Mrs. Norwood tells us that she serves them to her guests at teas, garden club parties and at her Christmas buffet. She warns us that if we serve Cucumber Sandwiches, we shouldn't expect to have any leftovers.

Mrs. Everett Meeks
Critics' Choice
The Guild of Corinth
Theatre Arts
Corinth
MISSISSIPPI

1 In a medium bowl, stir together the water, vinegar and salt. Add the cucumber slices and soak for 30 minutes. Drain the cucumbers and pat dry.

2 Using a 1½-to 2-inch round cookie or hors d'oeuvre cutter, cut the bread into shapes. Spread each shape lightly with butter.

3 In a small bowl, stir together the cream cheese and mayonnaise. Add the Worcestershire sauce, pepper and garlic salt. Spread the mixture onto the buttered side of the bread. Using a butter knife, spread the mixture smoothly and evenly.

4 Place 1 cucumber slice on top of the cream cheese mixture on half of the bread shapes. Place one of the remaining cream cheese mixture covered bread shapes on top of each of the cucumber slices, cream cheese side down. Press each sandwich gently together.

5 Place the sandwiches on a cookie sheet that has been covered with a slightly damp towel. Cover the

sandwiches with another slightly damp towel, then cover with plastic wrap. Chill for at least 3 hours before serving. Refrigerate leftover sandwiches for up to two days.

 TIPS FROM OUR KITCHEN

For a change of pace, cut these sandwiches into fanciful shapes, such as stars or diamonds. Just be sure to match the size of your cookie or hors d'oeuvre cutter to the size of your cucumber slices.

Use your imagination to decorate the sandwiches. Bits of fresh dill, pimiento and red pepper, and slices of fresh cucumber add flavor and color.

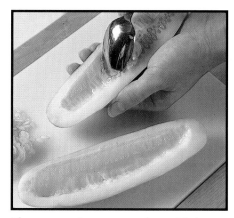

If you are using a cucumber with large seeds, cut the cucumber in half lengthwise and scoop out the seeds. Then slice the cucumber halves.

Nutrition Analysis *(Per Sandwich)*: Calories: 149 / Cholesterol: 20 mg / Carbohydrates: 14 g / Protein: 3 g / Sodium: 284 mg / Fat: 9 g (Saturated Fat: 4 g) / Potassium: 80 mg.

CUCUMBER SANDWICHES

CHILLED SHRIMP WITH HERBED CHEESE FILLING

CHILLED SHRIMP WITH HERBED CHEESE FILLING

Makes About 60 Appetizers

1¼	teaspoons salt
1	teaspoon ground red pepper
½	teaspoon black pepper
½	teaspoon dried thyme, crushed
½	teaspoon dried rosemary, crushed
½	teaspoon paprika
⅛	teaspoon dried oregano, crushed
2	cloves garlic, minced
2	pounds large, raw shrimp in shells
1	cup finely snipped parsley
2	3-ounce packages cream cheese, softened
2	tablespoons lemon juice
⅛	teaspoon white pepper

♦ ♦ ♦

Josephine Griswold, owner of The Willson-Walker Restaurant, told us about the restaurant's library of recipes from which she believes this recipe originated. This appetizer is a superb example of the historic restaurant's many delicious offerings.

The Willson-Walker Restaurant
<u>*Historic Lexington Cooks*</u>
<u>*Rockbridge Regional Recipes*</u>
Historic Lexington Foundation
Stonewall Jackson House
Lexington
VIRGINIA

1 In a Dutch oven, combine 8 cups *water*, *1 teaspoon* of the salt, the red pepper, black pepper, thyme, rosemary, paprika, oregano and *half* of the minced garlic; heat to boiling.

2 Meanwhile, rinse the shrimp. Add the shrimp to the boiling water. Reduce heat and simmer, uncovered, for 1 to 3 minutes or until the shrimp turn pink. Drain and cool.

3 In a small bowl, combine the parsley, cream cheese, lemon juice, the remaining minced garlic, the remaining salt and the white pepper. Mix well; transfer to a pastry bag fitted with a star tip.

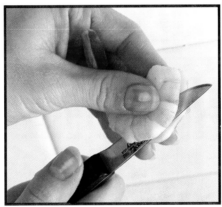

4 Peel the shrimp, leaving the tails intact. Devein each of the shrimp by using a sharp knife to make a shallow slit along the back from the head end to the tail. Rinse the shrimp under cold, running water to remove the vein, using the tip of a knife to lift it out, if necessary. Then, use the knife to make a deeper slit along the shrimp's back; *do not cut through.*

5 Pipe the cream cheese filling into each of the shrimp along the slit. Place the filled shrimp on several small serving platters, cover and chill for at least 1 hour.

 TIPS FROM OUR KITCHEN

Using a food processor is an easy way to snip the parsley finely. After processing the parsley, remove it from the processor bowl, then use the processor to blend the cream cheese filling.

Food safety is important. Prepare small plates of the shrimp, cover them and keep refrigerated until serving time. Then, set out just one plate at a time. To keep the food cold, nestle the serving plate on a bed of crushed ice. Any uneaten shrimp that have been at room temperature for two hours or more should be discarded.

Nutrition Analysis (*Per Appetizer*): Calories: 115 / Cholesterol: 19 mg / Carbohydrates: 0 g / Protein: 2 g / Sodium: 38 mg / Fat: 1 g (Saturated Fat: 0 g) / Potassium: 28 mg.

SHRIMP BALLS

Makes 24 Appetizers
1   medium onion, quartered
2   slices lemon
1   sprig parsley
1   pound fresh *or* frozen shrimp
     in shells
2   ounces cream cheese, softened
¼   cup finely chopped celery
2   tablespoons finely chopped
     green sweet pepper
1   tablespoon chili sauce
1   tablespoon grated onion
3   tablespoons snipped parsley
2   teaspoons prepared horseradish
1   teaspoon Worcestershire sauce
1   hard-cooked egg, chopped
Dash ground red pepper
3   tablespoons finely chopped
     pecans

♦   ♦   ♦

*Bell's Best is now in its third
edition, and it has been a tremen-
dous success. The book has sold
more than 350,000 copies, gen-
erating funds for many of the
Telephone Pioneers of America's
community service projects. Recipes
were contributed by friends, family
and members of the organization.*

Jeanette Boyd
Bell's Best
Telephone Pioneers of America
Mississippi Chapter No. 36
Jackson
MISSISSIPPI

1 Place 6 cups *water* in a large sauce-pan. Stir in the quartered onion, lemon slices, parsley sprig and 1 teaspoon *salt*; bring the mixture to a boil. Add the shrimp. Return the mixture to a boil; cook for 1 to 3 minutes or until the shrimp turn pink. Drain, shell and devein the shrimp. Place the shrimp in a bowl; chill.

2 Chop the shrimp into very fine pieces and place in a large bowl. Add the cream cheese, celery, green sweet pepper, chili sauce, grated onion, *1 tablespoon* of the parsley, the horse-radish, Worcestershire sauce, chopped egg and ground red pepper; mix well.

3 Shape the shrimp mixture into 1-inch balls (chill before shaping, if necessary to hold shape). Then roll the balls in a mixture of the chopped pecans and the remaining snipped parsley. Place the balls on baking sheets lined with waxed paper. Cover and chill until serving time.

 TIPS FROM OUR KITCHEN

You'll need about 1½ cups of cooked and shelled shrimp for this recipe.

To shell the shrimp: Carefully make a shallow cut lengthwise down the body, cutting just through the shell. Hold the shrimp in one hand; starting at the head end, carefully peel the shell back and away from the shrimp. Leave the last section of the shell and the tail intact. Gently pull on the tail portion to remove the entire shell.

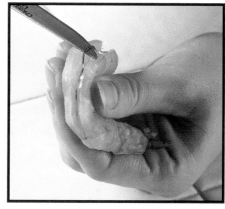

To remove the vein: Make a shallow slit with a sharp knife along the back of the shrimp. Use the tip of the knife to scrape out the black vein.

You can finely chop the shelled and deveined shrimp in a food processor, but to avoid turning the shrimp into paste, process by using several on and off pulses.

To serve and keep these appetizers cold, set the serving plate in a container of crushed ice. Discard any of these appetizers that are kept at room temperature longer than 2 hours.

Nutrition Analysis (*Per Appetizer*): Calories: 30 / Cholesterol: 33 mg / Carbohydrates: 1 g / Protein: 3 g / Sodium: 52 mg / Fat: 2 g (Saturated Fat: 1 g) / Potassium: 42 mg.

SHRIMP BALLS

STUFFED CHERRY TOMATO HALVES

STUFFED CHERRY TOMATO HALVES

Makes 40 to 60 Appetizers
- 20 to 30 cherry tomatoes
Cream Cheese Filling:
- 1 8-ounce package cream cheese, softened
- ¼ cup catsup *or* hot-style catsup
- 1 teaspoon dried dillweed
Guacamole Filling:
- 1 large ripe avocado, seeded and peeled
- 4 teaspoons lemon juice
- 1 tablespoon finely chopped onion
- 1 clove garlic, minced
Toppings:
- ½ of a 4½-ounce can whole tiny shrimp, drained
- 6 slices bacon, cooked and crumbled

♦   ♦   ♦

The Feingold Association is a support group that conducts research on the effects of certain foods and food additives on behavior and learning and provides information about its findings to members. <u>Made with Love, Not Additives</u> was put together to raise funds for research and education, as well as to present delicious additive-free recipes.

<u>*Made with Love, Not Additives*</u>
Feingold Association of the U.S.
Alexandria
VIRGINIA

1 Wash and stem the tomatoes. Cut each in half crosswise.

2 Using a melon baller or grapefruit spoon, scoop out the seeds and discard. Lay the tomatoes, cut side down, on paper towels. Let stand for 30 minutes.

3 To prepare the Cream Cheese Filling: In a small bowl stir together the cream cheese, catsup or hot-style catsup and dillweed until blended. Set aside.

4 To prepare the Guacamole Filling: In a small bowl, mash the avocado with a fork. Stir in the lemon juice, onion and garlic.

5 Using 2 spoons, pile about *1 teaspoon* of the desired filling in each tomato half. Garnish each of the tomato halves stuffed with the Cream Cheese Filling with a shrimp. And, garnish the tomato halves stuffed with the Guacamole Filling with crumbled bacon.

6 Cover and refrigerate up to 4 hours. Drain, if necessary, and serve on chilled plates.

TIPS FROM OUR KITCHEN

The number of tomatoes you need depends on which filling you want to use. Use about 30 whole tomatoes for the Cream Cheese Filling (makes 60 appetizers) and about 20 whole tomatoes for the Guacamole Filling (makes 40 appetizers).

Look for a very ripe avocado for the Guacamole Filling. To encourage fast ripening of a less-than-ripe avocado, place it in a clean brown paper bag or next to other fruit and check the ripeness in a day or two.

Both fillings can also be served as a dip with chips or as a spread on crackers or thinly sliced bread.

Canned crabmeat can be substituted for the shrimp.

To add extra zip, mix about ½ teaspoon of prepared horseradish into the Cream Cheese Filling, or a dash of hot pepper sauce into the Guacamole Filling.

Nutrition Analysis (*Per Appetizer*): Calories: 40 / Cholesterol: 10 mg / Carbohydrates: 1 g / Protein: 1 g / Sodium: 54 mg / Fat: 3 g (Saturated Fat: 2 g) / Potassium: 76 mg.

WORLD'S BEST DEVILED EGGS

Makes 24 Servings

12	eggs
½	cup mayonnaise *or* salad dressing
2	tablespoons finely chopped onion
1	teaspoon snipped fresh chives
1	teaspoon snipped parsley
1	teaspoon dry mustard
½	teaspoon paprika
½ to ¾	teaspoon dried dillweed
¼	teaspoon salt
¼	teaspoon pepper
¼	teaspoon garlic powder

Milk

❖   ❖   ❖

When the cookbook <u>Cause to Cook</u> *was being created, two very similar recipes for Deviled Eggs were submitted by Cindy Thury Smith and Marge Jacoboski. Cindy tells us that her version and Marge's often "turn up" at the same local parties. Cindy's grandmother passed down her recipe for deviled eggs to Cindy, who then adapted it to create World's Best Deviled Eggs.*

Cindy Thury Smith and

Marge Jacoboski

<u>Cause to Cook</u>

Jerry's Friends

Lilydale

MINNESOTA

1 Place the eggs in a large saucepan. Add enough cold water to cover. Bring the water to a rapid boil over high heat.

2 Reduce the heat so the water is just below simmering. (The water should have bubbles on the bottom of the pan with only a few rising to the top.) Cover and cook for 15 minutes.

3 Pour off the hot water; fill the pan with cold water and a few ice cubes. Let stand at least 2 minutes.

4 Pour off the water, then gently roll the eggs around by shaking the pan from side to side. This will crack the shells thoroughly and uniformly.

5 Remove the shells by starting to peel from the largest end of the egg. If the shell doesn't come off easily, hold the egg under running water while pulling away the shell.

6 Cut the eggs in half lengthwise and remove the yolks. Place the yolks in a shallow bowl and mash with a fork. Add the mayonnaise or salad dressing, onion, chives, parsley, dry mustard, paprika, dillweed, salt, pepper and garlic powder to the egg yolks. Stir. If necessary, stir in a little milk to achieve the desired consistency.

7 Spoon the yolk mixture into egg white halves. Cover and chill until serving time.

 TIPS FROM OUR KITCHEN

Don't be concerned if a greenish ring surrounds the yolk of a hard-cooked egg. This is a common, harmless occurrence caused by the formation of iron sulfide during the cooking process. To decrease the chances of this occurring, follow the above method of cooking.

When serving, do not leave eggs at room temperature for more than two hours. Deviled eggs may be kept in the refrigerator for up to one week.

Nutrition Analysis *(Per Serving)*: Calories: 73 / Cholesterol: 109 mg / Carbohydrates: 1 g / Protein: 3 g / Sodium: 80 mg / Fat: 6 g (Saturated Fat: 1 g) / Potassium: 38 mg.

WORLD'S BEST DEVILED EGGS

Salsa

Makes 4 Cups

3	whole tomatoes, chopped
½	4-ounce can green chilies, chopped (*or* more, depending on desired level of heat)
½	cup chopped onion
¼	cup sliced ripe olives
1	clove garlic, minced
1	tablespoon snipped fresh cilantro (*or* more, depending on desired level of heat)
¼ to ½	teaspoon bottled hot pepper sauce

◆ ◆ ◆

When the San Jose Auxiliary put together their cookbook <u>Under the Willows</u>, *they requested and received recipes from auxiliary members and their friends and families. This recipe was donated by the Diabetes Society of Santa Clara Valley. Thanks to all of the contributions, the cookbook has sold approximately 2,000 copies.*

Diabetes Society of Santa Clara Valley
<u>Under the Willows</u>
San Jose Auxiliary to the Lucile Salter Packard Children's Hospital at Stanford
San Jose
CALIFORNIA

1 In a blender container or food processor bowl, combine *half* of the tomatoes, *half* of the chilies, *half* of the onion, *half* of the olives, *half* of the minced garlic, *half* of the cilantro and *half* of the hot pepper sauce. Blend or process until the mixture is almost smooth.

2 Add the remaining tomatoes, chilies, onion, olives, garlic, cilantro and hot pepper sauce. Blend or process just until the ingredients are combined.

 TIPS FROM OUR KITCHEN

For a thicker salsa, use 2 pounds of plum-shaped tomatoes, such as Roma tomatoes. For a chunkier salsa, omit the blending or processing and simply stir the ingredients together.

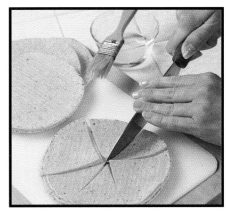

If you wish, you can serve this fat-free dip with low-fat, no-salt-added homemade tortilla chips. To make tortilla chips: Lightly brush flour or corn tortillas with cooking oil and stack them, oil side up. Cut the stacked tortillas into 8 wedges. Separate the wedges and spread them on baking sheets. Bake the tortilla wedges in a preheated 350° oven about 10 minutes or until the chips are crisp and just starting to brown.

Cilantro, also known as Chinese parsley, is the leaf portion of the coriander plant. It has a distinctive pungent, almost musty odor and flavor. Freshly picked small immature leaves have the best flavor. To grow your own coriander plant, plant the seeds as soon as the danger of frost has passed. Plants will grow from 2 to 3 feet tall in moderately rich, well-drained soil in full sun to partial shade.

Nutrition Analysis (*Per Tablespoon*): Calories: 3 / Cholesterol: 0 mg / Carbohydrates: 0 g / Protein: 0 g / Sodium: 6 mg / Fat: 0 g (Saturated Fat: 0 g) / Potassium: 15 mg.

JEANNE'S EGGPLANT APPETIZER

Makes 5½ Cups (About 22 Servings)

1 large eggplant, washed, peeled and cut into ½-inch cubes (6 cups)
½ cup olive oil
1 cup chopped onion
1 cup chopped celery
1 cup chopped green sweet pepper
1 cup tomato puree
¾ cup red wine vinegar
½ cup chopped ripe olives
2 tablespoons sugar
½ teaspoon salt

♦   ♦   ♦

Judy Elbaum, a free-lance cooking instructor, said she likes to serve Jeanne's Eggplant Appetizer on toasted pita bread, toast points or crackers. She credits her friend, Jeanne Katz, as the originator of the recipe. Judy submitted this recipe to the Candle Lighters's cookbook to help support Stepping Stones, a learning program for developmentally delayed children.

Judy Elbaum
Our Favorite Quick & Easy
Recipes
The Candle Lighters
Livingston
NEW JERSEY

1 In a 12-inch skillet over medium heat, cook the eggplant in the hot olive oil about 10 minutes or until it is lightly browned, stirring occasionally. Cover the skillet during the last 2 minutes of cooking to steam and soften the eggplant.

2 Add the onion, celery and green sweet pepper to the skillet. Cook and stir until the vegetables are crisp-tender. Stir in the tomato puree, red wine vinegar, olives, sugar and salt. Simmer, uncovered, for 10 minutes, stirring occasionally. Remove from the heat; cool.

3 Transfer the eggplant mixture to a covered container. Refrigerate overnight. Serve with toasted French bread rounds or toasted pita wedges.

TIPS FROM OUR KITCHEN

This dish is also delicious served over chicken, pork or fish.

Store this eggplant appetizer in the refrigerator up to 1 week or in the freezer up to 3 months. For quick identification, be sure to label the covered containers.

Package the mixture in a decorative container to give as a gift along with a loaf of cocktail bread and instructions for storing and serving.

Nutrition Analysis (*Per Serving*): Calories: 69 / Cholesterol: 0 mg / Carbohydrates: 6 g / Protein: 1 g / Sodium: 120 mg / Fat: 6 g (Saturated Fat: 1 g) / Potassium: 163 mg.

JEANNE'S EGGPLANT APPETIZER

SIX-LAYER PARTY DIP

SIX-LAYER PARTY DIP

Makes 16 Servings

1	cup dairy sour cream
1	cup mayonnaise
1	1¼-ounce envelope taco seasoning mix
1	large avocado, peeled and seeded
¼	cup salsa
2	tablespoons lemon juice
¼	teaspoon bottled hot pepper sauce
1	16-ounce can refried beans
½	teaspoon bottled hot pepper sauce
1½	cups shredded cheddar cheese (6 ounces)
1 to 2	tomatoes, chopped
1	4½-ounce can chopped ripe olives, well drained

Tortilla chips

♦　♦　♦

Elaine Morris, chairperson for McAlpin's Department Store Christmas Charities, told us about one way that McAlpin's brings joy to people in need at Christmas. On Christmas morning, the store hosts a special breakfast for the area's needy, after which guests are treated to a pre-paid $50 to $100 shopping spree.

Grace R. Costanzo
Seasoned With Love
McAlpin's Crestview Hills
Crestview Hills
KENTUCKY

1 In a small bowl, stir together the sour cream, mayonnaise and taco seasoning mix. Set aside.

2 In another bowl, mash the avocado with a fork. Stir in the salsa, lemon juice and the ¼ teaspoon bottled hot pepper sauce. Set aside.

3 In another bowl, stir together the refried beans and the ½ teaspoon bottled hot pepper sauce.

4 In a 2-quart rectangular glass baking dish, spread the bean mixture. Layer with the avocado mixture and then the sour cream mixture.

5 Sprinkle the cheese over the sour cream mixture. Top with the chopped tomatoes and sprinkle with the olives. Cover and refrigerate overnight. Serve with tortilla chips.

TIPS FROM OUR KITCHEN

For a dip with a less salty flavor, use only half of the taco seasoning mix.

For lower fat and fewer calories, use reduced-fat sour cream and mayonnaise.

To make your own tortilla chips, first stack corn or flour tortillas, then cut the tortilla stack into 6 wedges.

In a heavy saucepan or deep skillet, heat ½ inch *cooking oil* or *shortening*. Fry the tortilla wedges, a few at a time, until they are crisp and lightly browned (about 1 minute for corn tortillas or about 45 seconds for flour tortillas). Drain well on paper towels.

Nutrition Analysis (*Per Serving*): Calories: 388 / Cholesterol: 26 mg / Carbohydrates: 28 g / Protein: 8 g / Sodium: 744 mg / Fat: 29 g (Saturated Fat: 8 g) / Potassium: 324 mg.

MARY'S CHEESE BALL

Makes 3½ cups

1 8-ounce package cream cheese, softened
4 ounces blue cheese, finely crumbled
½ cup finely chopped onion
2 tablespoons prepared mustard
1 to 2 tablespoons pickle relish
2 teaspoons Worcestershire sauce
1 teaspoon prepared horseradish
½ teaspoon salt
2 cups shredded Swiss cheese, (8 ounces)
1 cup shredded cheddar cheese, (4 ounces)
1 tablespoon chili powder or paprika (optional)
½ cup ground walnuts or pecans (optional)
⅓ cup snipped fresh parsley or dill (optional)

♦ ◆ ♦

The call went out in Wilmington, to help restore the Grand Opera House. From the most popular fund-raising events sponsored by the Grand Opera Guild—their catered opening-night parties—came the superb cookbook Grand Recipes.

Jean M. Watkins
Grand Recipes
Grand Opera House Guild
Wilmington
DELAWARE

1 In a large bowl, combine the cream cheese with the blue cheese, onion, mustard, pickle relish, Worcestershire sauce, horseradish and salt. Beat the mixture with an electric mixer until it is light and fluffy. Fold in the Swiss and cheddar cheeses. Chill the cheese mixture for at least 2 hours.

2 Form the chilled cheese mixture into 1 large or 2 small balls.

3 Roll the cheese ball(s) in your choice of coatings: chili powder or paprika, walnuts or pecans, or parsley or dill. Wrap and chill until serving time, for up to 3 days.

 TIPS FROM OUR KITCHEN

To make the cheese ball(s) ahead of time, we suggest preparing the recipe through Step 2. Wrap the cheese ball(s) tightly in freezer-safe plastic wrap and freeze. The day before serving, place the ball(s) in the refrigerator to thaw. Just before serving, roll in the coating of your choice. This will keep the coatings nice and crunchy.

If you'd like, garnish with sprigs of fresh rosemary and whole strawberries. We suggest serving Mary's Cheese Ball with fresh cut-up fruit and vegetable crudités, breadsticks, flatbreads and a variety of crackers.

Nutrition Analysis *(Per Tablespoon):* Calories: 46 / Cholesterol: 12 mg / Carbohydrates: 1 g / Protein: 2 g / Sodium: 94 mg / Fat: 4 g (Saturated Fat: 2 g) / Potassium: 21 mg.

MARY'S CHEESE BALL

SALMON HORS D'OEUVRES

SALMON HORS D'OEUVRES

Makes 18 to 20 Appetizer Servings

1	14½-ounce can red salmon, drained, flaked and skin and bones removed
2	stalks celery, finely chopped
½	cup mayonnaise *or* salad dressing
1	tablespoon lemon juice
½	teaspoon onion powder
½	teaspoon celery seed
⅛	teaspoon pepper
1	pimiento-stuffed green olive
4	pitted ripe black olives, halved and thinly sliced
¼	teaspoon paprika

Lettuce
Parsley
½   lemon, thinly sliced
Crackers

◆   ◆   ◆

Twenty-five years ago, thirteen dedicated women created Forum Feasts as a fund-raiser to build a school for developmentally impaired children. Since then, the cookbook has sold over 320,000 copies, and continues to generate funds for the Forum School. Nancy Flower, chairperson, says that the cookbook project "started as a fund-raiser and has really turned into a labor of love."

Mrs. Richard D. Major

Forum Feasts

Waldwick

NEW JERSEY

1 In a medium mixing bowl, combine the salmon, celery, mayonnaise or salad dressing, lemon juice, onion powder, celery seed and pepper. (If desired, add *1 to 2 tablespoons* additional mayonnaise for a creamier mixture.)

2 On a serving plate, pat the mixture into the shape of a fish. Or, pat the mixture into a plastic wrap-lined 2- or 3-cup fish mold. Unmold onto a serving plate.

3 Decorate the fish, using the pimiento-stuffed green olive for the eye and the pitted black olive slices for scales. Sprinkle with the paprika.

4 Encircle the fish with lettuce and parsley. Garnish with twisted lemon slices. Cover and chill until ready to serve. Serve with crackers.

TIPS FROM OUR KITCHEN

To make the lemon twists: Cut halfway through a thin lemon slice, then twist one cut side. If desired, notch the peel before twisting and add a bit of red pimiento to the twist point.

If you're concerned about fat content, look for no-fat or low-fat labels on the mayonnaise or salad dressing. Check the fat content of your crackers as well.

If you don't have a fish mold or another fancy mold and don't want to hand shape the fish, you can use a 2-cup bowl lined with plastic wrap. Decorate the serving platter with ruffled lettuce, celery leaves, parsley and twisted lemon or lime slices.

Nutrition Analysis (*Per Serving*): Calories: 82 / Cholesterol: 13 mg / Carbohydrates: 1 g / Protein: 5 g / Sodium: 171 mg / Fat: 7 g (Saturated Fat: 1 g) / Potassium: 105 mg.

chapter two

hot
hors d'oeuvres

Light up the night with a delectable assortment of warm appetizers. Eye-catching Mushroom Tarts, savory Teriyaki Meat Sticks, and succulent Lea's Swedish Meatballs are merely a sampling of the tempting goodies in this chapter. Want to wow your guests? Chinese Baked Pork Rolls will surely captivate them. Need an inviting nibble for a summertime soirée? Crispy Zucchini Spears are a finger-licking way to use this garden staple. Looking for a make-ahead marvel? Spinach Empanadas can go from freezer to serving tray in just minutes. Spotlight one or dazzle with a selection—either way, these hot hors d'oeuvres are certain to captivate your audience.

CHICKEN-ALMOND PUFFS

CHICKEN-ALMOND PUFFS

♦ ♦ ♦

The Friends of the Library and the University Women's Club produced a superb cookbook in order to raise funds to purchase books for the University of Colorado Libraries-Boulder. All of the contributed recipes were carefully tested in home kitchens, including Nona Jahsman's Chicken-Almond Puffs. Nona tells us that these treats are always included in her cocktail party fare.

Nona Jahsman
The Colorado Cook Book
University of Colorado Women's
Club–Boulder
Friends of the Library
Boulder
COLORADO

1 Preheat the oven to 450°. Grease a baking sheet. Set aside.

2 In a saucepan over low heat, heat the butter or margarine and broth until the butter or margarine has melted.

3 In a small bowl, stir together the flour and salt. Add the flour mixture all at once to the saucepan. Stir vigorously over low heat until the mixture forms a ball and pulls away from the sides of the saucepan. Remove the pan from heat and cool for 5 to 10 minutes.

4 Add the eggs one at a time, beating thoroughly after each addition. Continue beating until a thick glossy dough is formed. Stir in the chicken, almonds and paprika.

5 Drop by small teaspoonfuls onto the prepared baking sheet. Bake in the 450° oven for 10 minutes. Reduce the heat to 350° and bake for 5 to 10 minutes more or until the puffs are golden brown.

TIPS FROM OUR KITCHEN

Toast the almonds by spreading them in a shallow baking pan. Bake in a 350° oven for 5 to 10 minutes or until golden brown, stirring once.

Be sure to let the dough cool before adding the eggs. If the dough is too hot, the eggs may overcook and prevent the puffs from becoming puffy and light.

To make evenly rounded puffs, use the same amount of dough for each one. Use another spoon or spatula to push the dough off the spoon onto the baking sheet. Don't go back and add more dough the original mound.

Nutrition Analysis (*Per Puff*): Calories: 38 / Cholesterol: 24 mg / Carbohydrates: 2 g / Protein: 1 g / Sodium: 53 mg / Fat: 3 g (Saturated Fat: 1 g) / Potassium: 19 mg.

Spinach Empanadas

Makes 60 Empanadas

Pastry:

2	8-ounce packages cream cheese, softened
¾	cup butter *or* margarine, softened
2½	cups all-purpose flour
½	teaspoon salt

Filling:

¼	cup finely chopped onion
3	cloves garlic, minced
4 to 5	slices bacon, cooked and crumbled (reserve 1 tablespoon bacon drippings)
1	10-ounce package frozen chopped spinach, thawed and drained
1	8-ounce container cottage cheese (1 cup)
¼	teaspoon pepper
⅛	teaspoon ground nutmeg
1	egg, beaten

♦   ♦   ♦

Anne Mitchell of Hickory, North Carolina, is justifiably proud of her Spinach Empanadas, which she says she's been making for as long as she can remember. Make and freeze a batch or two ahead of time for special occasions.

Anne Mitchell
<u>Market to Market</u>
Service League of North
Carolina, Inc.
Hickory,
NORTH CAROLINA

1 To make the pastry: In a large mixing bowl, beat together the cream cheese and the butter or margarine with an electric mixer until smooth. Gradually beat in the flour and salt. Knead the dough lightly by hand. Cover the dough with plastic wrap and refrigerate for 3 hours.

2 To make the filling: In a medium skillet, cook the onion and garlic in the reserved bacon drippings for 3 to 4 minutes or until the onion is tender but not brown. Stir in the crumbled bacon, the spinach, cottage cheese, pepper and nutmeg. Let the mixture cool.

3 Preheat oven to 450°.

4 On a lightly floured surface, roll out the pastry until it is ⅛ inch thick. Using a 3-inch biscuit cutter, cut out as many pastry circles as possible. Place *1 teaspoon* of the filling on one half of *each* pastry circle. Moisten the edges of the circle with the egg and fold the other half of the circle over the filling.

5 Place the pastries on ungreased baking sheets. Gently seal the edges of the empanadas with the tines of a fork. Brush the empanadas with the egg. Use the tines of a fork to prick a small vent in each. Bake in the 450° oven for 10 to 12 minutes or until the empanadas are golden.

TIPS FROM OUR KITCHEN

Because the mixture of cream cheese and butter is a heavy one, we recommend using a stand mixer instead of a hand-held mixer.

If you wish, serve these tasty little pastries with salsa.

Nutrition Analysis *(Per Empanada):* Calories: 76 / Cholesterol: 19 mg / Carbohydrates: 4 g / Protein: 2 g / Sodium: 92 mg / Fat: 6 g (Saturated Fat: 3 g) /Potassium: 34 mg.

SPINACH EMPANADAS

MINI CALZONES

MINI CALZONES

Makes About 30 Appetizers
- ¾ cup ricotta cheese
- ¼ cup grated Parmesan cheese
- 1 pound loaf frozen bread dough, thawed
- 1½ ounces thinly sliced pepperoni, cut in half
- 2 tablespoons milk
- 1 cup tomato sauce
- 1 teaspoon dried Italian seasoning

♦ ♦ ♦

The Benjamin F. Sullivan Unit #155—a unit of the American Legion Auxiliary—created and developed Cookbook Unit #155 to generate funds to help purchase supplies for the local homeless shelter. The organization is also involved with projects that benefit abused, missing and handicapped children, as well as with drug abuse prevention programs.

Gloria Schilling
Cookbook Unit #155
Benjamin F. Sullivan Unit #155
Pittsfield
MASSACHUSETTS

1 Preheat the oven to 375°. Grease 2 baking sheets and set aside.

2 In a small bowl, stir together the ricotta cheese and Parmesan cheese.

3 On a lightly floured surface, with a lightly floured rolling pin, roll the dough to slightly less than a ¼-inch thickness.

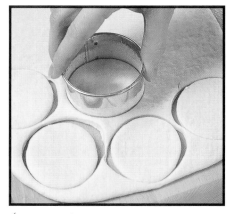

4 With a 2½-inch round cutter or drinking glass, cut out circles of the dough.

5 Place a generous *teaspoon* of the ricotta mixture and *½ slice* of pepperoni on half of each circle of the dough. Fold the circles in half and seal the edges by pressing with the tines of a fork.

6 Place the filled calzones on the prepared baking sheets. Prick the tops with a fork to allow steam to escape. Brush the tops with the milk. Bake in the 375° oven for 15 to 20 minutes or until golden.

7 Meanwhile, in a small saucepan, combine the tomato sauce and the Italian seasoning. Heat to boiling; reduce heat and simmer, covered, for 15 minutes.

8 Remove the calzones from the baking sheets. Serve immediately with the tomato sauce for dipping.

 TIPS FROM OUR KITCHEN

Calzones are a type of Italian turnover. The filling may be meat, cheese or vegetables.

If you're in a hurry, use 2 tubes of refrigerator pizza dough instead of frozen bread dough. The pizza dough may open a little more during baking, but the filling won't ooze out and you'll save quite a bit of time. Both doughs will be easier to roll if you let them rest a few minutes occasionally during rolling. Likewise, before re-rolling the dough scraps, press them together and let the new ball rest a few minutes.

The dough will be easier to fold over the filling if the cut (straight) edge of the pepperoni half slice is at the fold line. It also may be necessary to stretch the dough a bit to cover the filling.

Nutrition Analysis: (*Per Appetizer*): Calories: 75 / Cholesterol: 4 mg / Carbohydrates: 10 g / Protein: 3 g / Sodium: 163 mg / Fat: 3 g (Saturated Fat: 1 g) / Potassium: 62 mg.

MUSHROOM TARTS

Dorothy O'Neill says that Mushroom Tarts are a treat her family loves. Dorothy saves preparation time by making these appetizers in steps, often making the shells ahead of time and freezing them. Then shortly before serving time, Dorothy makes the filling.

Dorothy O'Neill
Create Share Enjoy!
The Saint Joseph's Christian
Women's Society
Brookfield
WISCONSIN

1 Preheat the oven to 400°.

2 To make the pastry shells: In a medium mixing bowl, stir together the flour and salt. Using a pastry blender, cut in the butter or margarine until the pieces are the size of small peas. Slowly add the ice water until the mixture is moist enough to form a ball.

3 On a floured surface, roll the dough to a ¼-inch thickness. Using a 3-inch-round cookie cutter, cut the dough into circles. Re-roll scraps, if necessary.

4 Place the dough rounds over the bottoms (outsides) of 1¾-inch muffin cups. Firmly press the dough around the cups.

5 Bake in the 400° oven for 10 to 12 minutes or until the shells are lightly browned. Cool slightly, then remove from the pans.

6 To make the filling: In a large skillet, melt *2 tablespoons* of the butter or margarine. Add the onion and cook until tender but not brown. Add the remaining butter, the mushrooms and lemon juice. Cover and cook for 5 minutes over medium heat. Drain, if necessary; set aside.

7 In a saucepan, heat the whipping cream until it just starts to boil. Add the salt and pepper. In a small bowl, stir together the cornstarch and water; slowly stir the mixture into the hot cream. Cook and stir until the cornstarch mixture is thickened. Stir in the mushroom mixture. Remove from heat. Spoon the filling into the tart shells and sprinkle with the cheese.

8 Place the tarts in a shallow baking pan. Broil 4 to 5 inches from the heat for 2 to 3 minutes or until the tarts are puffed and the cheese melts.

 TIPS FROM OUR KITCHEN

If you don't have a pastry blender, you can use 2 table knives to cut in the butter. Hold one knife in each hand and draw the knives across each other.

If you wish, garnish the tarts with sliced green olives.

Nutrition Analysis (*Per Appetizer*): Calories: 117 / Cholesterol: 27 mg / Carbohydrates: 7 g / Protein: 2 g / Sodium: 110 mg / Fat: 9 g (Saturated Fat: 6 g) / Potassium: 74 mg.

MUSHROOM TARTS

VEGETABLE MUSHROOM CAPS

VEGETABLE MUSHROOM CAPS

Makes 8 Servings

24	large fresh mushrooms (about 1½ to 2 inches in diameter)
2	tablespoons butter *or* margarine
½	cup finely chopped onion
½	cup finely chopped celery
2	teaspoons Worcestershire sauce
1	tablespoon snipped regular *or* Italian parsley
¼	teaspoon salt
⅛	teaspoon pepper
2	tablespoons butter *or* margarine, melted
	Regular *or* Italian parsley sprigs (optional)

Thymes Remembered presents an intimate portrait of food, drawn from the most cherished family occasions. This recipe for Vegetable Mushroom Caps is one example of the many unique delectables found in the cookbook compiled by The Junior League of Tallahassee. This dynamic group of women is committed to promoting volunteerism and community improvement.

Thymes Remembered
The Junior League of
Tallahassee, Inc.
Tallahassee
FLORIDA

1 Rinse the mushrooms and pat dry. Remove and chop the stems. Set the mushroom caps aside.

2 Melt the 2 tablespoons butter or margarine in a large skillet. Stir in the mushroom stems, onion, celery, Worcestershire sauce, parsley, salt and pepper. Cook and stir until the vegetables are tender.

3 Brush the mushroom caps with the melted butter or margarine and spoon in the vegetable mixture.

4 Place the caps, stuffed side up, in the skillet. Cover and cook over medium heat for 8 minutes.

5 Transfer the mushroom caps from the skillet to a warm platter. Garnish with parsley, if desired.

 TIPS FROM OUR KITCHEN

If you want to enjoy your guests instead of being stuck in the kitchen, try baking these caps rather than frying them. Arrange the mushroom caps in a 15x10x1-inch baking pan. Bake in a 425° oven for 8 to 10 minutes or until heated through.

Nutrition Analysis (*Per Serving*): Calories: 85 / Cholesterol: 15 mg / Carbohydrates: 7 g / Protein: 3 g / Sodium: 149 mg / Fat: 6 g (Saturated Fat: 4 g) / Potassium: 473 mg.

LEA'S SWEDISH MEATBALLS

Makes 30 to 32 Appetizer Servings

1	pound lean ground beef
8	ounces ground pork
¾	cup fine dry bread crumbs
½	cup finely chopped onion
½	cup milk
1	egg
1	tablespoon snipped parsley
1	teaspoon Worcestershire sauce
1	teaspoon salt
⅛	teaspoon pepper
¼	cup cooking oil
1	8-ounce carton dairy sour cream
¼	cup all-purpose flour
½	teaspoon salt
⅛	teaspoon pepper
2	cups water

◆   ◆   ◆

Even though Linda Goode wasn't able to tell us who Lea was, she remembered that she received the recipe from her mother-in-law. Linda said that this was an hors d'oeuvre her mother-in-law "always served at our New Year's Day open house." She also noted that these meatballs are easy to make and they serve a crowd of people.

Linda Goode
Central Texas Style
Junior Service League
of Killeen, Inc.
Killeen
TEXAS

1 In a large bowl, stir together the ground beef, ground pork, bread crumbs, onion, milk, egg, parsley, Worcestershire sauce, the 1 teaspoon salt and the ⅛ teaspoon pepper; mix well. Shape the mixture into 64 walnut-size balls.

2 In a 12-inch skillet, heat the cooking oil. Add *half* the meatballs and cook for 12 to 15 minutes or until no pink remains, turning the meatballs to brown them evenly. Remove the meatballs from skillet; set aside. Repeat. Reserve the drippings in the skillet.

3 In a small bowl, stir together the sour cream, flour, the ½ teaspoon salt and the ⅛ teaspoon pepper. Add the water; mix well. Stir the mixture into the drippings in the skillet; heat until the gravy is thickened and bubbly.

4 Add the meatballs to the gravy in the skillet and heat through.

 TIPS FROM OUR KITCHEN

Crumble 3 slices of bread in your food processor to make the bread crumbs for this recipe.

One medium onion chopped in a food processor will yield enough onion for this recipe.

To brown the meatballs evenly on all sides, use a 12-inch skillet and turn the meatballs constantly. This also helps to keep them evenly rounded.

You can also brown and bake the meatballs in the oven. To bake the meatballs: Place them in a single layer in a 15x10x1-inch baking pan. Bake in a 350° oven for 15 to 20 minutes or until no pink remains. Then, stir together the flour and sour cream in a skillet or chafing dish; stir in the water. Add the meatballs and heat through.

If you're serving these meatballs at a buffet, be sure to keep them hot to prevent bacteria from growing.

Nutrition Analysis (*Per Serving*): Calories: 89 / Cholesterol: 24 mg / Carbohydrates: 3 g / Protein: 5 g / Sodium: 147 mg / Fat: 6 g (Saturated Fat: 2 g) / Potassium: 76 mg.

LEA'S SWEDISH MEATBALLS

CHINESE BAKED PORK ROLLS

CHINESE BAKED PORK ROLLS

Makes 12 Servings
Marinade:

- 2 tablespoons soy sauce
- 2 tablespoons catsup
- 1 tablespoon sugar
- 1 tablespoon dry white wine
- 1 tablespoon vinegar
- 1 teaspoon cornstarch
- 1 teaspoon toasted sesame oil
- ⅛ teaspoon pepper
- 1 pound pork tenderloin

Stuffing:

- 6 dried mushrooms
- 4 whole scallions
- 8 water chestnuts

♦   ♦   ♦

Residents, staff and family members at the St. Cabrini Nursing Home had the opportunity to work together on a cookbook designed to raise funds for the Nursing Home. Madame Yee Yo, author of <u>You Can Cook Anything Chinese</u>, contributed her recipe for Chinese Baked Pork Rolls to the cause because her parents, Mr. and Mrs. Wan Tze, were both residents of St. Cabrini for years.

Madame Yee Yo
<u>*Cabrini Cares*</u>
St. Cabrini Nursing Home
Dobbs Ferry
NEW YORK

1 To make the marinade: In a medium bowl, stir together the soy sauce, catsup, sugar, white wine, vinegar, cornstarch, sesame oil and pepper.

2 Cut the pork tenderloin crosswise into 12 thin slices. With a meat mallet, pound each piece between sheets of heavy-duty plastic wrap to a ¼-inch thickness. Toss the meat in the marinade and let stand for 15 minutes.

3 Preheat the oven to 400°.

4 To make the stuffing: Soak the mushrooms in *boiling water* for 15 minutes. Drain; discard the water and the stems. Thinly slice the mushrooms lengthwise. Using a knife, cut the scallions into thin shreds. Chop the water chestnuts. Stir together the vegetables.

5 Remove the pork slices from the marinade and drain, reserving the marinade. Place *2 tablespoons* of the stuffing on each pork slice. Roll the slice of pork around the stuffing. Fasten each roll with a wooden toothpick. Arrange the rolls in a single layer in a baking dish. Pour the reserved marinade over the pork rolls. Bake in the 400° oven for 20 minutes.

TIPS FROM OUR KITCHEN

To shred scallions or green onions: Trim off the root ends and tops, leaving about 4 inches of green. Place the trimmed scallions on a cutting board and thinly slice them lengthwise, then cut them crosswise into 4-inch lengths.

Use heavy-duty plastic wrap to cover meat before pounding it. Lightweight plastic wrap or waxed paper is likely to tear as you pound.

If desired, the mushroom mixture can be made a day ahead and refrigerated until ready to use.

If you prefer, marinate the pork slices in the refrigerator up to two hours.

Nutrition Analysis (*Per Serving*): Calories: 68 / Cholesterol: 27 mg / Carbohydrates: 27 g / Protein: 9 g / Sodium: 207 mg / Fat: 2 g (Saturated Fat: 0 g) / Potassium: 224 mg.

GRILLED BACON-WRAPPED SHRIMP

Makes 8 Servings

- 2 cups hickory, apple *or* cherry wood chips
- ¼ cup water
- ¼ cup soy sauce
- 1 tablespoon brown sugar
- 1 tablespoon dry sherry
- 1 large clove garlic, crushed
- Dash Worcestershire sauce
- Dash ground red pepper
- ½-inch piece fresh gingerroot, peeled and grated
- 24 large shrimp (about 1 pound), shelled with tails left intact and deveined
- 8 slices lean bacon

◆　　◆　　◆

Combine an avid interest in grilling, an area boasting the freshest seafood and a generous-with-her-recipes aunt from Alabama and what you get (if you're as lucky as we are) is Tricia Willis's Grilled Bacon-Wrapped Shrimp.

Tricia Willis
Thymes Remembered
Junior League of Tallahassee
Tallahassee
FLORIDA

1 Cover the wood chips with water and soak for 30 minutes. Drain.

2 In a medium saucepan, combine all the remaining ingredients, *except* the shrimp and bacon. Cover and stir over medium heat to blend the flavors. Remove from heat; set aside to cool.

3 Place the shrimp in a medium bowl. Pour the marinade over the shrimp. Cover and chill for 1 to 2 hours, stirring occasionally.

4 Remove the shrimp from the marinade and drain well. Discard the marinade.

5 In a large skillet, partially cook the bacon until just limp. Drain on paper towels and cool.

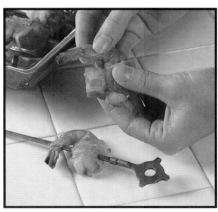

6 Cut each bacon slice into thirds. Wrap a piece of bacon around each shrimp and secure with a skewer.

7 Sprinkle wood chips over hot coals. Grill skewers of shrimp over hot coals for 6 to 10 minutes or until shrimp turns pink, turning once. Do not overcook.

◆

 TIPS FROM OUR KITCHEN

Because the bacon on these appetizers is only partially cooked, the dripping fat may cause some flare-ups during grilling. To combat flare-ups, raise the grill rack, cover the grill, space the coals farther apart or remove a few coals. If a large flare-up occurs, remove the appetizers from the grill and mist the fire with a pump-spray bottle filled with water. When the flare-up has died down, resume grilling.

To broil these appetizers, place the bacon-wrapped shrimp on a cold broiler rack. Cook 4 inches from the heat for 6 to 10 minutes or until done, turning once.

Nutrition Analysis (*Per Serving*): Calories: 95 / Cholesterol: 92 mg / Carbohydrates: 3 g / Protein: 12 g / Sodium: 716 mg / Fat: 4 g (Saturated Fat: 1 g) / Potassium: 139 mg.

GRILLED BACON-WRAPPED SHRIMP

TERIYAKI MEAT STICKS

Teriyaki Meat Sticks

Makes About 24 Meat Sticks

¼ cup packed brown sugar
¼ cup soy sauce
¼ cup sake *or* dry sherry
1 clove garlic, minced
¼ teaspoon ground ginger
¼ teaspoon monosodium
   glutamate (optional)
1 pound beef round steak,
   cut across the grain into
   ⅛-inch slices

❖   ❖   ❖

Teriyaki Meat Sticks are a popular Hawaiian "pu pu"—that's Hawaiian for hors d'oeurves—and everyone has a favorite recipe. Bobbe Johnson adds sherry to give hers a unique flavor. She skewers the marinated meat beforehand and sets the meat sticks out on a platter beside a tabletop hibachi. Then Bobbe invites her guests to gather round and grill their own appetizers. What could be easier?

Bobbe Johnson
Pupus from Paradise
Assistance League of Hawaii
Honolulu
HAWAII

1 Soak about twenty-four 6- or 8-inch bamboo skewers in cold water for 30 minutes. Drain.

2 Meanwhile, in a shallow bowl, stir together the brown sugar, soy sauce, sake or dry sherry, garlic, ginger and, if desired, monosodium glutamate. Add the beef slices. Cover and marinate at room temperature for 15 to 30 minutes.

3 Preheat the broiler or grill. Thread the beef slices accordion-style onto the bamboo skewers, reserving the marinade.

4 Place the skewers on a broiler pan and broil 4 to 6 inches from the heat for 3 to 4 minutes or until the meat reaches the desired doneness, basting occasionally with the marinade and turning once. Or, grill the meat sticks directly over medium coals for 4 to 5 minutes, basting occasionally with the marinade and turning once. Serve hot.

 TIPS FROM OUR KITCHEN

You can use this marinade to flavor and tenderize steaks and other cuts of beef for grilling.

If you want to reduce the sodium in this dish, use low-sodium soy sauce.

The round steak will be easier to slice if it is partially frozen. Freeze about 20 minutes, then slice.

Soaking the bamboo skewers prevents them from burning during cooking.

You can substitute 1 teaspoon freshly grated gingerroot for the ground ginger in this recipe.

Nutrition Analysis *(Per Meat Stick)*: Calories: 36 / Cholesterol: 12 mg / Carbohydrates: 1 g / Protein: 5 g / Sodium: 95 mg / Fat: 1 g (Saturated Fat: 0 g) / Potassium: 72 mg.

Makes 3 to 4 Servings
1⅓ cups all-purpose flour
1 tablespoon melted butter *or* margarine
2 egg yolks, beaten
¾ cup beer
2 egg whites, stiffly beaten
Cooking oil
1 pound fresh vegetables, sliced, halved *or* cut into strips (such as zucchini, yellow summer squash, onions *and/or* mushrooms)

◆   ◆   ◆

The Kona Outdoor Circle created <u>*Kona Kitchens*</u> *"to collect, document and share with residents and visitors alike a treasury of recipes which…represents the unique and diverse cookery of the Kona Coast." The cookbook consists of more than 845 original, adapted or time-honored recipes contributed by area residents. Each recipe was screened at taste-testing parties, and many of the recipes currently are used at their meetings.*

Richard Reichel
<u>*Kona Kitchens Award-Winning*</u>
<u>*Community Cookbook*</u>
Kona Outdoor Circle
Kailua-Kona
HAWAII

1 In a large bowl, stir together the flour, ½ teaspoon *salt* and ¼ teaspoon *pepper*. Stir in the melted butter or margarine and beaten egg yolks. Gradually add the beer until all of the ingredients are well blended. Cover the bowl and chill the batter up to 12 hours.

2 When ready to cook, carefully fold the beaten egg whites into the beer batter.

3 In a large skillet or wok, heat the cooking oil to 365°. Dip the prepared vegetables, one at a time, into the beer batter, allowing the excess batter to drain. Carefully place 2 or 3 pieces at a time in the skillet or wok. Cook for 3 to 5 minutes or until the vegetables are golden brown all over.

4 Using a slotted spoon or tongs, transfer the cooked vegetables to a paper towel-lined plate to drain. Repeat with the remaining vegetables. Serve the vegetables hot, sprinkled lightly with additional *salt*.

TIPS FROM OUR KITCHEN

Use a wire whisk or rotary beater to make a lump-free batter.

Choose a pan that is large enough to allow 1½ to 2 inches of cooking oil to bubble up when the vegetables are added.

Use a deep-fat frying thermometer to check the temperature of the hot cooking oil. For the best results, maintain a 365° temperature.

To minimize spattering, be sure the vegetables are thoroughly dried before coating them with the batter and frying them. Fry only a few pieces at a time. Use a slotted spoon or tongs to add and remove the vegetables.

Nutrition Analysis (*Per Serving*): Calories: 510 / Cholesterol: 294 mg / Carbohydrates: 48 g / Protein: 11 g / Sodium: 410 mg / Fat: 30 g (Saturated Fat: 7 g) / Potassium: 429 mg.

VEGETABLE FRITTERS

CRISPY ZUCCHINI SPEARS

CRISPY ZUCCHINI SPEARS

Makes 6 Servings

3	medium zucchini
⅓	cup yellow cornmeal
⅓	cup all-purpose flour
¼	cup grated Parmesan cheese
½	teaspoon onion powder
¼	teaspoon salt
⅛	teaspoon seasoned pepper
1	beaten egg
2	tablespoons milk
3	tablespoons margarine *or* butter, melted

♦   ♦   ♦

We spoke with Elizabeth Day's daughter, Marie Wienholft. She told us that her mother has the oven going all the time and that this dish is frequently requested by Elizabeth's family. Marie has a large garden, and she said that her mother always comes over to pick up fresh zucchini to use when she prepares this crispy addition to any meal.

Elizabeth Day
Immanuel Lutheran Church
Cookbook
Immanuel Lutheran Ladies Aid
Immanuel Lutheran Church
Michigan City
INDIANA

1 Preheat the oven to 450°. Lightly grease a 3-quart rectangular baking dish; set aside.

2 Cut off and discard the ends of the zucchini. Cut each zucchini in *half* horizontally. Slice *each* zucchini half lengthwise into quarters to make *24* spears total.

3 In a shallow dish or pie plate, stir together the cornmeal, flour, grated Parmesan cheese, onion powder, salt and seasoned pepper until well mixed. In another shallow dish or pie plate, stir together the beaten egg and milk.

4 Roll *each* zucchini spear in the cornmeal mixture, dip it into the egg mixture, then roll it again in the cornmeal

mixture; the spears should be completely coated with the cornmeal mixture.

5 Arrange the coated zucchini spears in a single layer in the prepared baking dish. Drizzle the spears with the melted margarine or butter. Bake in the 450° oven for 15 to 20 minutes or until the zucchini spears are golden and just tender.

 TIPS FROM OUR KITCHEN

For firmer zucchini spears, select small- to medium-size zucchini.

Freshly picked zucchini will keep in a plastic bag in the refrigerator up to 2 weeks. Purchased zucchini is best when used within 5 days. It is important to be sure that there is no moisture present on the zucchini or inside the bag before you place the zucchini in the refrigerator.

Nutrition Analysis (*Per Serving*): Calories: 174 / Cholesterol: 39 mg / Carbohydrates: 18 g / Protein: 5 g / Sodium: 249 mg / Fat: 9 g (Saturated Fat: 2 g) / Potassium: 211 mg.

ZIPPY POTATO SKINS

In 1909 the Stone Ridge Library was chartered in memory of Julia and Garret Hasbrouck. The Taster's Choice cookbook was created from popular dishes that were tasted for twenty-five cents at a booth at a local fair. The proceeds from the sales of the cookbook provided the community with the money to celebrate the 75th anniversary of the library.

Cookbook Committee
Taster's Choice
Stone Ridge Library
Stone Ridge
NEW YORK

1 Preheat the oven to 400°.

2 Thoroughly scrub the potatoes with a brush under cold running water. Pat the potatoes dry and prick each potato with a fork. Bake in the 400° oven about 1 hour or until the potatoes are tender.

3 In a small bowl, stir together the melted butter or margarine and hot pepper sauce; set aside.

4 Cut *each* potato in half lengthwise. Using a spoon, scoop out the potato pulp leaving a ¼-inch-thick shell, reserving the potato pulp for another use.

5 Cut each potato shell lengthwise into 1-inch-wide strips. Place the potato skin strips on a baking sheet.

6 Broil the potato skin strips 3 to 4 inches from the heat source about 5 minutes or until the strips are crisp. (Or, bake the strips in a 450° oven for 12 to 15 minutes or until crisp.) Transfer the baking sheet to a heat-proof surface; do not turn off the broiler (or oven).

7 Brush the skins with the butter mixture. Sprinkle with the Monterey Jack cheese. Return the baking sheet to the broiler; broil about 1 minute more or until the cheese melts. (Or, return the baking sheet to the oven for 3 to 4 minutes or until the cheese melts.) If desired, sprinkle with the crumbled bacon.

 TIPS FROM OUR KITCHEN

Russet potatoes are often recommended for baking because of their thick skins. Long white potatoes can be baked too, even though they have thin skins. Regardless of the type of potato you choose, be sure to select potatoes that are free of green spots or "eyes."

For a change of taste, substitute a Mexican-flavored hot sauce for the regular hot pepper sauce in this recipe.

Add a little milk and butter or margarine to the reserved potato pulp to turn it into mashed potatoes. Or, use the potato pulp to make potato bread, potato pancakes or potato soup.

Nutrition Analysis (*Per Serving*): Calories: 58 / Cholesterol: 7 mg / Carbohydrates: 8 g / Protein: 1 g / Sodium: 36 mg / Fat: 3 g (Saturated Fat: 2 g) / Potassium: 137 mg.

ZIPPY POTATO SKINS

soups

Wonderfully versatile, soup can tempt the palate, appease the appetite, or add to the culinary splendor of a meal—and you'll find just the right soup for any occasion in these pages. Serve refreshing Iced Red Pepper Soup to start a summer supper, or use rich Autumn Bisque as the centerpiece of a fall feast. If you need a wonderfully woodsy, easy treat, try Fresh Mushroom Soup. And for a truly special occasion, few dishes can compare with luscious Lobster Bisque, both for elegance and exquisite flavor.

CREAM OF CUCUMBER SOUP

CREAM OF CUCUMBER SOUP

Makes 8 Servings

- 4 large cucumbers (2 pounds)
- 3 tablespoons butter *or* margarine
- ½ cup finely chopped green onion
- 6 cups chicken broth (49½-ounce can)
- ¾ teaspoon dried dillweed
- ¼ cup farina (cream of wheat)
- 3 to 4 teaspoons tarragon vinegar
- ¼ teaspoon fresh ground pepper
- 1 cup light cream, half-and-half, dairy sour cream *or* crème fraîche
- Sliced cucumbers, snipped fresh dill *or* parsley (optional)

♦ ♦ ♦

More Than a Tea Party was such a success that the members of the Junior League of Boston recently sold the last copy and now they are thrilled with having to decide whether or not to reprint it. The cookbook was created to raise funds for the League's thirty community service projects.

More Than a Tea Party
The Junior League of Boston
Boston
MASSACHUSETTS

1 Peel the cucumbers. Slice the cucumbers in half lengthwise. Using a spoon, scoop out and discard the seeds. Slice the cucumber halves thinly; set aside.

2 In a Dutch oven, melt the butter or margarine. Add the green onion and cook over low heat until the onion is tender but not brown. Add the cucumbers; cook and stir for 1 to 2 minutes. Add the chicken broth and dillweed; heat to boiling. Stir in the farina. Reduce heat and simmer the mixture, uncovered, for 20 to 25 minutes.

3 Puree the mixture, *one-third* at a time, in a blender container or food processor bowl. Pour the pureed mixture into a bowl or covered container. Stir the tarragon vinegar and pepper into the cucumber mixture.

4 Cover and refrigerate about 4 hours or until the mixture is cool. Stir in the light cream, half-and-half, sour cream or crème fraîche. Cover and chill for 2 more hours or overnight. Serve the soup in chilled bowls or glass mugs. If desired, garnish the servings with cucumber slices, snipped dill or parsley.

TIPS FROM OUR KITCHEN

You'll want to use fresh cucumbers in this recipe. Fresh cucumbers are available year round. When shopping for cucumbers, look for those that are firm, without shriveled or soft spots. Smaller cucumbers of any type will be more tender. Fresh cucumbers can be stored in the refrigerator up to 2 weeks.

For a soup that is lower in calories and salt, reduced-calorie sour cream and reduced-sodium chicken broth can be substituted in this recipe.

To make Crème Fraîche: In a small bowl, stir together ½ cup *whipping cream* (not ultrapasteurized) and ½ cup *dairy sour cream*. Cover with plastic wrap. Let stand at room temperature for 2 to 5 hours or until the mixture is thickened. When thickened, cover and chill in the refrigerator until serving time or up to 1 week. Stir before serving.

Farina—also known as cream of wheat—is a mild-flavored wheat product. It is commonly found in hot breakfast cereals.

Nutrition Analysis (*Per Serving*): Calories: 150 / Cholesterol: 32 mg / Carbohydrates: 7 g / Protein: 6 g / Sodium: 641 mg / Fat: 11 g (Saturated Fat: 7 g) / Potassium: 410 mg.

ICED RED PEPPER SOUP

Makes 6 Servings

4	leeks (white part only)
4	large red sweet peppers, halved and seeded
3	tablespoons butter *or* margarine
3	cups chicken stock
¼	teaspoon dried thyme, crushed
2	bay leaves
1	cup Crème Fraîche *or* one 8-ounce carton dairy sour cream
¼	teaspoon white pepper
½	red sweet pepper, cut into very thin strips

◆　　◆　　◆

Years ago, Jean Landreth and her husband were traveling in Roven, France with Jean's friend—a French cooking teacher—and her husband. The two couples were visiting with friends, who were gourmet cooks, when they were lucky enough to taste Iced Red Pepper Soup. Now Jean makes the soup for family and friends, often using red sweet peppers from her own garden.

Jean Landreth
<u>Under the Willows</u>
San Jose Auxiliary to the Lucile
Salter Packard Children's
Hospital at Stanford
San Jose
CALIFORNIA

1 In the bowl of a food processor or by hand, chop the white part of the leeks and the 4 red sweet peppers.

2 In a 3-quart saucepan over low heat, melt the butter or margarine. Add the chopped leeks and red sweet peppers. Cover and cook about 15 minutes or until the vegetables are soft.

3 Carefully add *1 cup* of the chicken stock into the vegetable mixture. Add the thyme and bay leaves. Bring the mixture to a boil; reduce heat. Cover and simmer for 30 minutes. Remove and discard the bay leaves.

4 In a blender container or food processor bowl, puree the vegetable mixture, *half* at a time, until smooth. Strain the pureed mixture into a large bowl; discard the solids.

5 Stir the remaining chicken stock into the pureed vegetable mixture; cool.

6 Stir the Crème Fraîche or sour cream into the cooled vegetable mixture until the ingredients are well blended and no white streaks remain. Stir in the white pepper and *salt* to taste. Cover the bowl and refrigerate the soup for several hours or until it is chilled through.

7 Serve the soup in bowls, garnished with the red sweet pepper strips.

 TIPS FROM OUR KITCHEN

Crème Fraîche is made from whipping cream and a bacterial culture that causes the cream to thicken and develop a sharp, tangy flavor. It is softer and milder than sour cream. If you can't find it in your specialty store, here's a substitute: In a small bowl, stir together ½ cup *whipping cream* (not ultrapasteurized) and ½ cup *dairy sour cream*. Cover the bowl with plastic wrap; let stand at room temperature for 2 to 5 hours or until the mixture is thickened. Cover and chill until ready to use or up to 2 weeks. Stir before using.

This soup may be served hot as well as chilled. If you are serving the soup hot, you may want to increase the seasonings. *Do not* stir in the Crème Fraîche until just before serving.

Nutrition Analysis (*Per Serving*): Calories: 255 / Cholesterol: 70 mg / Carbohydrates: 13 g / Protein: 5 g / Sodium: 498 mg / Fat: 21 g (Saturated Fat: 13 g) / Potassium: 340 mg.

ICED RED PEPPER SOUP

GAZPACHO

GAZPACHO

6   medium tomatoes
1   medium cucumber, peeled, seeded and chopped
1   medium onion, finely chopped
1   medium green sweet pepper, finely chopped
1   clove garlic, minced
1½ cups tomato juice
¼   cup olive oil
2   tablespoons vinegar
1   teaspoon salt
¼   teaspoon pepper
Few drops of bottled hot pepper sauce
Croutons

♦   ♦   ♦

"You always look for something easy with eight kids!" Edie Hellman tells us. All of her children love this dish and Edie finds herself preparing it in large batches. She suggests that you serve Gazpacho on hot summer days when you want something cool, refreshing and hassle-free.

Edie Hellman
Home on the Range
Home on the Range
Sentinel Butte
NORTH DAKOTA

1 Bring a medium saucepan of water to a boil. Carefully plunge the tomatoes into the boiling water for 30 seconds to loosen the skins.

2 Immerse the tomatoes in cold water to cool quickly. Remove the skins.

3 Coarsely chop the tomatoes and place them in a large bowl. Add the cucumber, onion, green pepper and garlic. Stir in the tomato juice, olive oil, vinegar, salt, pepper and hot pepper sauce.

4 Cover the gazpacho and chill it at least 4 hours. Serve cold and sprinkle with croutons.

TIPS FROM OUR KITCHEN

For a zippier soup, substitute spicy tomato juice for the plain tomato juice.

Look for plump, well-shaped fresh tomatoes that are firm textured and bright colored for the variety. Avoid bruised, cracked or soft tomatoes. If fresh tomatoes need to ripen, store them at room temperature in a brown paper bag or in a fruit ripening bowl with other fruits. Don't stand them in the sun to ripen, or they will become mushy. When ripe, tomatoes will yield slightly to gentle pressure.

Nutrition Analysis *(Per Serving)*: Calories: 148 / Cholesterol: 0 mg / Carbohydrates: 16 g / Protein: 3 g / Sodium: 651 mg / Fat: 10 g (Saturated Fat: 1 g) Potassium: 539 mg.

Autumn Bisque

Makes 6 Servings

- 1 pound butternut squash, peeled, halved, seeded and cubed
- 2 tart apples, peeled, cored and cubed
- 1 medium onion, chopped
- 2 slices white bread, crusts removed and cubed
- 4 cups chicken broth
- ½ teaspoon salt
- ¼ teaspoon pepper
- ¼ teaspoon dried rosemary, crushed
- ¼ teaspoon dried marjoram, crushed
- 2 egg yolks, slightly beaten
- ¼ cup heavy whipping cream
- Thin apple slices (optional)
- Fresh rosemary (optional)

◆　　◆　　◆

Although Kim Button quadrupled her recipe for this hearty soup when she served it at a bazaar, there still wasn't enough to go around. Everyone loved it so much, it was gone within an hour! Kim makes this old family recipe every Thanksgiving and suggests that if you serve this to your guests, you should be prepared to share the recipe.

Kim Button
Kids Bowling for Kids Village
Cookbook
Seattle
WASHINGTON

1 In a large saucepan, combine the squash, apples, onion, bread, chicken broth, salt, pepper, rosemary and marjoram. Bring to boiling. Reduce heat and simmer, uncovered, about 35 minutes or until the squash and apples are tender. Remove from heat; cool slightly.

2 Spoon *one-third* of the soup into a blender container or food processor bowl. Cover and blend or process until puréed. Repeat with the remaining soup.

3 Return all of the puréed mixture to the saucepan. Reheat the soup gently over very low heat.

4 In a small bowl, stir together the egg yolks and whipping cream. Beat in *1 cup* of the hot soup, then add the yolk mixture to the saucepan, stirring constantly. Heat and stir just until the soup begins to boil.

5 Transfer the soup to a tureen. Garnish with the apple slices and rosemary, if desired.

Tips from Our Kitchen

Adding a small portion of the hot soup to the egg yolk and cream mixture warms the egg and cream so it will be less likely to form lumps when combined with the rest of the hot soup.

Depending on the variety of squash you choose, you might find the squash easier to handle if you first cut the squash into halves or quarters, then remove the seeds. Finally cut off the flesh from the peel and cube.

Instead of the butternut squash, experiment with other winter squashes such as acorn, banana, turban, hubbard and buttercup. When shopping, choose a squash that is heavy for its size and has a hard rind.

Nutrition Analysis *(Per Serving)*: Calories: 138 / Cholesterol: 49 mg / Carbohydrates: 17 g / Protein: 5 g / Sodium: 746 mg / Fat: 6 g (Saturated Fat: 3 g) / Potassium: 386 mg.

68

AUTUMN BISQUE

LOBSTER BISQUE

LOBSTER BISQUE

Makes 6 to 8 Servings

- 1   11- or 12-ounce can lobster (about 2 cups)
- ¼   cup butter *or* margarine
- 1   medium onion, chopped (½ cup)
- ½   cup all-purpose flour
- 2   14½-ounce cans chicken broth
- ¾   cup dry sherry
- 3   cups light cream *or* half-and-half
- 2   teaspoons tomato paste
- Dash pepper
- Wheat crackers (optional)

◆   ◆   ◆

Although Lobster Bisque can be "thrown together," Carole Wainscott calls this her "loving recipe" because in order for it to taste best, "you really must take your time." She usually begins simmering the ingredients in the morning, then refrigerates the finished bisque and reheats it right before serving. The finished product is definitely well worth the "loving" you put into it.

Mrs. Carole Wainscott
Marvelous Dining
Auxiliary to the Marion County Medical Society, Inc.
Indianapolis
INDIANA

1 Drain the lobster. Remove and discard any bony pieces. Set aside several pieces of lobster for a garnish; chop the remaining lobster.

2 In a large saucepan or 4-quart Dutch oven, melt the butter or margarine. Add the onion; cook and stir until soft. Stir in the flour. Add the chicken broth all at once. Cook and stir until the mixture is thickened and bubbly. Cook and stir for 2 minutes more.

3 Add the chopped lobster and the dry sherry. Bring to a boil.

4 Gradually stir in the light cream or half-and-half, tomato paste and pepper. Heat through.

5 To serve, ladle the soup into bowls. Garnish with the reserved lobster pieces. Serve with wheat crackers, if desired.

TIPS FROM OUR KITCHEN

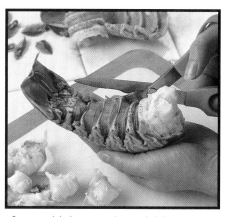

If canned lobster isn't available, use two 8-ounce frozen lobster tails. Look for packages that are intact with no evidence of ice or juices. The meat should have no dry or frosty areas. Cook the thawed lobster tails in a large pot of boiling water for 8 to 12 minutes or until the shells are bright red and the meat is tender. Remove the lobster tails from the boiling water, drain and allow to cool enough to handle. Remove the lobster meat from shells and cut up. Using kitchen shears, cut away the softer meat under the shell along each side.

For a less rich—and lower calorie—soup, substitute milk for part of the cream.

Nutrition Analysis (*Per Serving*): Calories: 637 / Cholesterol: 222 mg / Carbohydrates: 16 g / Protein: 18 g / Sodium: 792 mg / Fat: 53 g (Saturated Fat: 33 g) / Potassium: 481 mg.

CREAM OF ARTICHOKE SOUP

Makes 8 Side-Dish Servings

2 large *or* 3 medium artichokes
2 bay leaves
1 tablespoon lemon juice
¼ cup finely chopped onion
¼ cup finely chopped celery
3 tablespoons butter *or* margarine
3 tablespoons all-purpose flour
3 cups chicken broth
2 tablespoons lemon juice
¼ teaspoon salt
¼ teaspoon dried thyme, crushed
⅛ teaspoon white pepper
⅛ teaspoon grated nutmeg (optional)
¾ cup milk
¼ cup dairy sour cream
1 egg yolk, beaten
Dairy sour cream (optional)
Fresh thyme (optional)

♦   ♦   ♦

The Junior League of Palo Alto compiled A Private Collection to raise funds for their many community projects.

A Private Collection
The Junior League of Palo Alto/ Mid Peninsula
Menlo Park
CALIFORNIA

1 Cover the artichokes with *salted water*. Add *1* of the bay leaves and the 1 tablespoon lemon juice. Simmer for 35 to 40 minutes or until the artichokes are very tender. Drain and cool.

2 Remove the chokes and discard. Scrape the meat from the leaves. Reserve the meat and discard the leaves. Chop the artichoke bottoms. Set aside.

3 In a large saucepan, cook and stir the onion and celery in the butter or margarine until the vegetables are tender.

4 Add the flour. Cook and stir for 1 minute. Add the chicken broth and the 2 tablespoons lemon juice all at once. Add the artichoke meat and chopped artichoke bottoms, the remaining bay leaf, the salt, thyme, white pepper, and nutmeg (if using). Cover and simmer for 20 minutes. Cool slightly. Puree *half* at a time in a blender or food processor.

5 In a small bowl, stir together the milk, sour cream and egg yolk.

6 Return the pureed mixture to the saucepan; bring to a boil. Remove from heat and add the milk mixture, beating briskly with a wire whisk.

7 Return the saucepan to the heat and cook for 2 minutes more; *do not boil.* Serve the soup immediately, or cool and refrigerate to serve cold. If desired, garnish with a dollop of sour cream and fresh thyme.

 TIPS FROM OUR KITCHEN

Early spring is the peak harvest time for fresh artichokes. Look for compact, firm globes that are heavy for their sizes. Place in a plastic bag and refrigerate. Fresh artichokes will keep up to a week, but the flavor is best when used within two days.

If desired, garnish each serving of soup with a thin lemon slice and a bit of minced parsley. Since this is such a special soup, you may want to make special lemon slices by cutting out small triangles in the peel.

Nutrition Analysis (*Per Serving*): Calories: 128 / Cholesterol: 44 mg / Carbohydrates: 11 g / Protein: 6 g / Sodium: 480 mg / Fat: 8 g (Saturated Fat: 4 g) / Potassium: 350 mg.

CREAM OF ARTICHOKE SOUP

FRESH MUSHROOM SOUP

FRESH MUSHROOM SOUP

Makes 6 to 8 Servings

¼	cup butter *or* margarine
12	ounces sliced fresh mushrooms (4½ cups)
1 to 2	cloves garlic, minced
¼	cup all-purpose flour
2	cups chicken broth
2	cups milk
½	cup snipped parsley
¼	teaspoon salt
⅛	teaspoon ground nutmeg
⅛	teaspoon pepper
3	tablespoons dry vermouth (optional)

◆   ◆   ◆

Tandy Sweeney Graves told us that her mother has always had a great influence on her cooking. In fact, it was when she and her mother were "playing around with different recipes" fifteen years ago that they created Fresh Mushroom Soup. Tandy likes to entertain, but says it's difficult to find the time to prepare the food. This dish is an easy and delicious solution.

Tandy Sweeney Graves
<u>Magic</u>
*The Junior League
of Birmingham*
**Birmingham
ALABAMA**

1 In a large saucepan, melt the butter or margarine. Add the mushrooms and garlic to the saucepan; cook and stir for 5 minutes.

2 Stir in the flour, blending well. Slowly add the broth, followed by the milk. Bring to a boil, stirring constantly.

3 Reduce the heat and simmer for 5 minutes. Add the parsley, salt, nutmeg and pepper. Add the vermouth, if desired, and cook until the mixture is heated through.

 TIPS FROM OUR KITCHEN

To reheat a single serving of the soup: Place 1 serving (¾ cup) in a microwave-safe bowl. Cover and micro-cook on 100% power (high) for 2 to 3 minutes or until heated through, stirring once.

Using whole milk will add richness. If you want an even richer flavor, use half-and-half. For a heartier soup, add 1 cup cooked wild rice.

You may want to experiment to find the flavor you like best by using different types of mushrooms. The common white, cream and brown mushrooms, with their familiar umbrella shape, have a mild flavor. The chanterelle (shant uh REL) has a golden to yellow-orange color and a delicate, meaty flavor. Oriental varieties

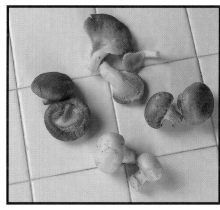

of mushrooms include: the enoki (ee KNOCK ee), a variety with a very mild flavor; the oyster with its pale cream to gray color and mild flavor; and the shiitake (shih TOCK ee) with its large floppy caps and rich, meaty flavor. (Shiitake stems are not used.)

Nutrition Analysis (*Per Serving*): Calories: 144 / Cholesterol: 22 mg / Carbohydrates: 11 g / Protein: 6 g / Sodium: 472 mg / Fat: 9 g (Saturated Fat: 5 g) / Potassium: 454 mg.

CREAM OF CARROT SOUP

Makes 8 to 10 Servings

2	tablespoons margarine *or* butter
1	small onion, chopped (⅓ cup)
5 to 6	medium carrots, peeled and chopped (3 cups)
1	large potato, peeled and cubed
2	14½-ounce cans chicken broth
1½	cups chopped fresh mushrooms
1	stalk celery, chopped
1	clove garlic, minced
½	teaspoon sugar
½	teaspoon salt
½	teaspoon dried thyme, crushed *or* 1½ teaspoons fresh snipped thyme
¼	teaspoon bottled hot pepper sauce
½	cup milk

Dairy sour cream (optional)
Fresh thyme sprigs (optional)

◆   ◆   ◆

Claire Bielawa tells us that her mother-in-law gave her this recipe. When Claire's family has their Easter dinners, this colorful and delicious soup is the dish that the children like best.

Claire M. Bielawa
The Mark Twain Library
Cookbook
The Mark Twain Library
Association
Redding
CONNECTICUT

1 In a large saucepan, melt *1 table-spoon* of the margarine or butter. Add the onion and cook until tender and light brown.

2 Add the carrots and potato. Cook and stir for 2 minutes. Carefully add the chicken broth, mushrooms, celery, garlic, sugar, salt, thyme and hot pepper sauce. Bring to a boil, then reduce the heat. Cover and simmer about 50 minutes or until the vegetables are very tender.

3 Let the soup mixture cool slightly, then transfer about *one-third* of the mixture to a blender container. Cover and blend until smooth. Repeat with the remaining mixture. Return the entire mixture to the saucepan.

4 Stir in the milk and the remaining margarine or butter. Heat the soup thoroughly, but do not boil. Season to taste with additional *salt* and *pepper*, if desired. Ladle the soup into individual bowls. Garnish with sour cream and fresh thyme, if desired.

 TIPS FROM OUR KITCHEN

Chopping the vegetables helps them to cook faster and blend into the liquid more smoothly.

Using a food processor is a quick way to chop the vegetables. You can also use a food processor to puree the cooked mixture. Process about *one-third* of the total mixture at a time.

For soup with a similar color but a different flavor, substitute 3 cups squash chunks for the carrots.

Nutrition Analysis (*Per Serving*): Calories: 101 / Cholesterol: 1 mg / Carbohydrates: 13 g / Protein: 4 g / Sodium: 569 mg / Fat: 4 g (Saturated Fat: 1 g) / Potassium: 391 mg.

CREAM OF CARROT SOUP

first course
salads

Starter salads are a little bit lighter and slightly smaller than the main-course variety. These days, a salad can be made with an incredible variety of ingredients, and our salads showcase this diversity. For a new twist on an old favorite, try Bacon, Lettuce and Tomato Salad. And Asparagus with Raspberry Vinaigrette is a sensational yet simple start to a special meal. Other first-act offerings include Wright's Raspberry Gorgonzola Salad, Orange-Kiwi-Avocado Salad, and Stuffed Artichokes—all intriguingly delicious.

BACON, LETTUCE AND TOMATO SALAD

Makes 6 Servings
Lettuce leaves
4 large ripe tomatoes
Salt
1 pound fresh mushrooms, sliced (6 cups)
12 strips bacon, crisply cooked and crumbled coarsely
4 green onions with tips, thinly sliced
⅓ cup salad oil
2 tablespoons red wine vinegar
½ teaspoon garlic salt
⅛ teaspoon freshly ground pepper
Finely shredded Swiss *or* mozzarella cheese, *or* grated Parmesan cheese

◆ ◆ ◆

The cookbook One of a Kind *is one of the major fund-raisers for the Junior League of Mobile, Inc.* One of a Kind *is marketed in all fifty states and in Canada. Profits from sales have been used in the past to help the league with its projects on substance abuse and education.*

Betty Jean Megginson
One of A Kind
The Junior League of Mobile, Inc.
Mobile
ALABAMA

1 Rinse the lettuce leaves under cool running water and pat dry with paper towels or dry in a salad spinner. Arrange the lettuce leaves, divided equally, on 6 plates.

2 Cut *18* thin slices from *3* of the tomatoes. Lightly salt the tomato slices. Arrange *3* tomato slices on *each* lettuce-lined plate.

3 Coarsely chop the remaining tomato. In a medium bowl, toss together the chopped tomato, mushrooms, bacon, green onions, salad oil, red wine vinegar, garlic salt and pepper.

4 Spoon the tossed salad, divided equally, over the tomato slices. Sprinkle with the shredded Swiss, mozzarella or grated Parmesan cheese, sprinkling only 1 kind of cheese.

TIPS FROM OUR KITCHEN

Use the best flavored tomatoes you can find. Yellow or red work equally well. Cherry or plum-shaped tomatoes also can be used. If using plum-shaped tomatoes, consider cutting 1 only part of the way through to make a fan-shaped garnish.

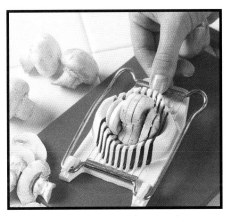

When you have quite a few mushrooms to slice, using an egg slicer saves a lot of time.

Turn this salad into a complete meal by adding boiled shrimp, lump crabmeat or cubed cooked chicken or turkey. Then serve with a selection of whole grain breads.

To serve at a potluck, line a large platter with the lettuce leaves and arrange the vegetables and bacon on top. Then sprinkle some Swiss, mozzarella or Parmesan cheese over all.

Nutrition Analysis (*Per Serving*): Calories: 255 / Cholesterol: 19 mg / Carbohydrates: 9 g / Protein: 9 g / Sodium: 432 mg / Fat: 22 g (Saturated Fat: 6 g) / Potassium: 579 mg.

AVOCADO SALAD WITH ARTICHOKE DRESSING

Makes 4 Servings

- 1 6-ounce jar marinated artichoke hearts
- 1 to 3 tablespoons fresh lemon juice
- 1 teaspoon Dijon-style mustard
- 2 cloves garlic, minced
- ¼ teaspoon dried tarragon, crushed
- ⅛ teaspoon salt
- 1 to 2 dashes bottled hot pepper sauce
- ¼ cup olive oil
- 1 small head romaine, washed, core removed and torn into bite-size pieces (about 6 cups)
- ¼ small head red cabbage, shredded (about 2 cups)
- 1 medium ripe avocado, pitted, peeled and thinly sliced

♦   ♦   ♦

Wigh Cook? was compiled in honor of Msgr. John J. Wigh, the founding pastor of the St. Gregory the Great Home and School Association. Proceeds from cookbook sales were used to purchase a retirement gift for Msgr. Wigh and to help support the school that he established.

Diane Fortier
Wigh Cook?
St. Gregory the Great
Home & School Association
Danbury
CONNECTICUT

1 In a blender container or food processor bowl, combine the *undrained* artichoke hearts, lemon juice, Dijon-style mustard, garlic, tarragon, salt and hot pepper sauce.

2 Cover and blend or process until smooth. With the machine running, add the oil in a thin, steady stream. (This should take about 1 minute.) Continue blending or processing until the mixture is smooth and thick. Transfer the dressing to a small bowl or glass jar, cover and refrigerate.

3 To serve the salad, divide the romaine and cabbage among 4 chilled plates. Spoon on the desired amount of dressing and arrange the avocado slices on top. Serve immediately. Chill any leftover dressing and use within 48 hours.

 TIPS FROM OUR KITCHEN

You may find different avocado varieties in your store. The oval-shaped, rich-flavored *Hass* and the pear-shaped, milder-flavored *Fuerte* come from California. More than 65 varieties of avocado come from Florida. All avocados have a delicate, nutty flavor. The interior fruit is hard like an apple when unripe, but turns to a buttery texture when ripe.

Knowing how you intend to use an avocado will help you choose the right one when shopping. For this salad you'll want one that is firm-ripe for slicing. Avocados that are very ripe are best used for guacamole or other recipes that call for mashing.

Very firm avocados will ripen at room temperature in 3 to 4 days. To encourage faster ripening, place the avocado in a clean brown paper bag or next to other fruit. To slow down ripening, store ripe avocados in the refrigerator and use within a few days. Freezing ruins the texture of avocados.

Avocados are easier to peel if cut in half first. Hold one half, cut side down, and use a sharp paring knife to peel away the skin.

Nutrition Analysis (*Per Serving*): Calories: 248 / Cholesterol: 0 mg / Carbohydrates: 9 g / Protein: 3 g / Sodium: 243 mg / Fat: 25 g (Saturated Fat: 2 g) / Potassium: 667 mg.

AVOCADO SALAD WITH ARTICHOKE DRESSING

WILTED SPINACH SALAD AND DRESSING

WILTED SPINACH SALAD AND DRESSING

Makes 6 Servings
- 1 pound fresh spinach, torn into bite-size pieces (12 cups)
- 4 ounces fresh mushrooms, sliced
- 3 slices bacon, crisply cooked and crumbled

Dressing:
- ¼ cup cider vinegar
- 2 tablespoons sugar
- 1 teaspoon dry mustard
- ¼ teaspoon salt
- ¼ teaspoon dried oregano, crushed
- Dash garlic powder
- Dash pepper
- ½ cup salad oil
- ¼ cup chopped red onion
- 2 hard-cooked eggs, sliced

◆　◆　◆

Ellie Mayfield's mother gave her this terrific recipe for Wilted Spinach Salad and Dressing. Ellie found the recipe to be a wonderful way to entice young children to eat spinach. She also said that for quite awhile, she was making this dish for every dinner party—in fact, she was making the salad so often, she decided she just had to start trying other recipes!

Ellie Mayfield
What's Cooking in Philadelphia
The Philadelphia Rotary Club
Philadelphia
PENNSYLVANIA

1 In a large salad bowl, toss together the spinach, mushrooms and bacon; set aside.

2 To make the dressing: In a medium mixing bowl, combine the cider vinegar, sugar, dry mustard, salt, oregano, garlic powder and pepper. Beating constantly with an electric mixer, gradually add the salad oil. Transfer the dressing to a small saucepan. Cook and stir over medium heat until the dressing is hot.

3 Pour the hot dressing over the spinach salad. Toss to mix all of the ingredients and to wilt the spinach. Garnish the salad with the red onion and egg slices.

 TIPS FROM OUR KITCHEN

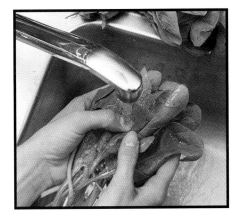

Look for fresh spinach with dark green leaves that are crisp and free of moisture or mold. Avoid spinach with broken or bruised leaves. Thoroughly rinse the spinach under cold running water to remove any sand.

To micro-cook the bacon: Place the bacon on a microwave-safe rack or paper plate. Cover with paper towels and cook on 100% power (high) for 2 to 3 minutes.

The dressing will separate after standing so only make the amount you need just before serving.

Nutrition Analysis (*Per Serving*): Calories: 253 / Cholesterol: 74 mg / Carbohydrates: 10 g / Protein: 7 g / Sodium: 249 mg / Fat: 22 g (Saturated Fat: 4 g) / Potassium: 749 mg.

WRIGHT'S RASPBERRY GORGONZOLA SALAD

Makes 8 to 10 Servings

Dressing:
- 1 cup olive oil
- ½ cup raspberry vinegar
- ¼ cup honey
- 1 teaspoon poppy seed
- 1 teaspoon dried mint, crushed
- ½ teaspoon dry mustard
- ½ teaspoon salt

Salad:
- 3 cups shredded red cabbage
- 8 cups torn Bibb lettuce
- 8 cups torn escarole
- 1 sweet red pepper, cut into julienne strips
- 1 medium red apple, sliced
- 8 ounces Gorgonzola cheese, crumbled

❖ ❖ ❖

Many of the recipes that still grace the menu of the 100-year-old Wright's Seafood Inn were created by Jan Davis's grandmother-in-law, Verne. Jan created this unusual Raspberry Gorgonzola Salad herself and tells us that it is a frequent choice of Wright's patrons.

Jan Davis
Wright's Seafood Inn
Three Rivers Cookbook
Child Health Association of Sewickley, Inc.
Sewickley
PENNSYLVANIA

1 To make the dressing: Place the olive oil, raspberry vinegar, honey, poppy seed, mint, mustard and salt in a jar with a tight-fitting lid. Shake well to combine.

2 To make the salad: First, shred the cabbage by cutting the head into quarters. Then place a quarter section, with a cut side down, on a cutting board. Hold a chef's knife perpendicular to the cabbage. Slice it into ⅛- to ¼- inch-thick shreds. Marinate the cabbage in *1 cup* of the dressing for 1 hour in the refrigerator.

3 Wash the Bibb lettuce and escarole. Dry and place in a large salad bowl. Keep the bowl in the refrigerator until ready to serve.

4 Just before serving, drain the cabbage, reserving the dressing.

5 Toss the lettuce with enough of the dressing to coat the greens. Arrange the salad on individual plates. Top with the red cabbage, red pepper strips and apple slices.

6 Sprinkle with the crumbled Gorgonzola cheese.

 TIPS FROM OUR KITCHEN

To crumble Gorgonzola: Hold the cheese in place with one fork and crumble an edge with another.

Save some of this raspberry dressing to serve over a fresh fruit salad.

For a change of pace, try substituting a green apple such as a Granny Smith.

Nutrition Analysis *(Per Serving)*: Calories: 411 / Cholesterol: 21 mg / Carbohydrates: 19 g / Protein: 8 g / Sodium: 550 mg / Fat: 36 g (Saturated Fat: 9 g) / Potassium: 490 mg.

WRIGHT'S RASPBERRY GORGONZOLA SALAD

FLORIDA SALAD

FLORIDA SALAD

Makes 8 Servings
- 4 cups torn spinach
- 2 cups torn endive *or* Boston lettuce
- 1 pint chilled mixed orange and grapefruit sections, drained
- 1 red onion, sliced

Dressing:
- ⅓ cup frozen grapefruit juice concentrate, thawed and undiluted
- ¼ cup water
- ¼ cup salad oil
- 1 tablespoon all-purpose flour
- 1 tablespoon wine vinegar
- 1 teaspoon sugar
- 6 slices bacon, cooked and crumbled

❖   ❖   ❖

Judy Toft has been part of the Chicago Mayfair Lioness Club for 23 years. She tells us that each year the members search for new ways to raise money for the Lions of Illinois Research Hospital. The first year, the club developed a cookbook. It was so successful that after some years, they decided to create another cookbook, The Art of Cooking in the 80s.

Al Juarez
The Art of Cooking in the 80s
Mayfair Lioness Club
Chicago
ILLINOIS

1 In a large salad bowl, toss together the spinach, endive or Boston lettuce, orange and grapefruit sections and red onion slices. Refrigerate the salad mixture while making the dressing.

2 To make the dressing: In a small saucepan, stir together the undiluted grapefruit juice concentrate, water, salad oil, flour, wine vinegar, sugar,

½ teaspoon *salt* and ¼ teaspoon *pepper*. Heat the mixture, stirring gently, until it begins to bubble. Cook and stir for 1 minute more. Remove from heat; stir in the crumbled bacon.

3 Pour the hot dressing over the salad mixture and toss to coat the ingredients with the dressing. Serve immediately.

 TIPS FROM OUR KITCHEN

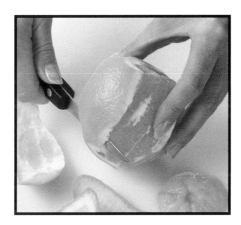

You can substitute 3 fresh oranges and 2 fresh grapefruits for the fruit sections

in this recipe. To section oranges and grapefruit: Cut a thin slice from *each* end of the fruit. Cut off the peel and white membrane with a very sharp utility knife or a specially designed serrated knife. Hold the fruit over a bowl to catch the juices. Cut between 1 fruit section and the membrane, cutting to the center of the fruit. Turn the knife and slide it up the other side of the section next to the membrane; repeat. Remove any seeds.

You'll need about 8 ounces of spinach and about 4 ounces of endive or Boston lettuce for this recipe. Wash the greens thoroughly; drain and place them in a plastic bag lined with paper towels. Store the greens in the refrigerator up to 3 days. Discard the stems when tearing the leaves.

This salad should be served as soon as it's made so that the spinach and lettuce leaves don't become too soggy.

Nutrition Analysis (*Per Serving*): Calories: 144 / Cholesterol: 4 mg / Carbohydrates: 13 g / Protein: 3 g / Sodium: 235 mg / Fat: 9 g (Saturated Fat: 2 g) / Potassium: 380 mg.

Orange-Kiwi-Avocado Salad

Makes 6 to 8 Servings
4   large oranges
Lime juice
¼   teaspoon salt
1   tablespoon honey
¼   walnut *or* salad oil
2   large avocados
4   kiwi fruit

♦   ♦   ♦

The Junior League of Phoenix, Arizona, which has been in existence since the 1930s, put together two cookbooks celebrating the eclectic cuisine of the Southwest. For each cookbook, they searched for recipes that would both reflect the local color and, of course, taste absolutely delicious. League member Polly Fitzgerald thinks the local efforts created a winning collection. Orange-Kiwi-Avocado Salad is one fabulous example.

Fiesta under the Sun
Junior League of Phoenix
Phoenix
ARIZONA

1 Peel the oranges. To section an orange, use a sharp paring knife to remove the white membrane. Working over a bowl to catch the juices, cut into the center of each orange between one section and the membrane. Turn the knife and cut along the other side of the section next to the membrane, as shown. Continue until all of the oranges are sectioned.

2 Measure the reserved orange juice. Add enough lime juice to make ½ cup. Add the salt, honey and oil. Beat the dressing with a wire whisk until it is combined.

3 Cut lengthwise through one avocado around the pit. With your hands, twist the avocado halves in opposite directions to separate them. Tap the pit with the blade of a sharp knife so that the knife catches in the pit. Carefully rotate the knife to loosen the pit. Lift the knife and remove the pit. Repeat with the second avocado. Slice the avocados. Peel and slice the kiwi fruit.

4 Arrange the orange sections and avocado and kiwi slices on salad plates. Drizzle *half* of the dressing over the salads. Serve the remaining dressing on the side.

 Tips from Our Kitchen

For an extra-special touch, serve this fruit salad on a bed of greens. Kale, salad savoy or romaine lettuce would be especially effective.

Naval oranges result in prettier sections because you don't have to remove seeds.

Nutrition Analysis *(Per Serving):* Calories: 246 / Cholesterol: 0 mg / Carbohydrates: 20 g / Protein: 2 g / Sodium: 99 mg / Fat: 19 g (Saturated Fat: 2 g) / Potassium: 622 mg.

ORANGE-KIWI-AVOCADO SALAD

ASPARAGUS WITH RASPBERRY VINAIGRETTE

Asparagus with Raspberry Vinaigrette

Makes 6 Servings

30	spinach leaves (about 3 cups)
30	asparagus spears, trimmed to 4½ inches
1	10-ounce package frozen raspberries with juice, thawed and drained
⅓	cup olive oil
¼	cup whipping cream
2	tablespoons vinegar
¼	teaspoon salt
⅛	teaspoon pepper

Fresh raspberries (optional)
Snipped fresh chives (optional)
Cracked black pepper (optional)

◆　◆　◆

Since 1972, the Novato Human Needs Center has been providing human services to the North Marin community. The center's programs include providing food and clothing assistance for those in need, a child abuse hotline, a parental stress hotline, a phone-friend hotline for latchkey children, a senior transportation program and an employment service program, among others.

Sue Cummings
Novato Human Needs
Center Cookbook
Novato Human Needs Center
Novato
CALIFORNIA

1 Wash and stem the spinach, then pat dry. Set aside.

2 In a Dutch oven, bring about 1 inch of *water* to a boil. Add the asparagus spears; cover and cook for 3 to 4 minutes or until the asparagus is crisp-tender. Place the asparagus in a colander and rinse with cold water. Set aside.

3 Place the raspberries in a blender container or food processor bowl. Cover and puree the berries. Strain the puree through a fine sieve into a bowl, discarding the seeds. Wash the blender container or food processor bowl.

4 Place the olive oil, whipping cream, vinegar, salt and pepper into the blender container or food processor bowl. Cover and blend or process until combined. Blend in the raspberry puree.

5 To serve: Arrange 5 spinach leaves on *each* of 6 plates. Arrange 5 asparagus spears on top of each bed of spinach. Pour about *2 tablespoons* of the raspberry vinaigrette mixture over the center of each serving. Garnish with raspberries, snipped chives and cracked pepper, if desired. Store any leftover dressing in the refrigerator up to 7 days.

Tips from Our Kitchen

This recipe makes about ¾ cup extra vinaigrette dressing, enough to dress any extra ingredients you might add to the recipe. For example, you might add red onion rings, cooked chicken, cubed melon, pea pods or orange segments. As

an alternative, you might like to save any leftover dressing to dress a fruit salad.

Fresh asparagus is most readily available in April and May. Choose straight and firm spears with good color and tightly closed buds. The spears will cook more evenly if they are all about the same diameter. To store asparagus up to four days, wrap the stems in wet paper towels, then place in a tightly sealed plastic bag and refrigerate. Just before using asparagus, wash and cut or break off the stem ends.

Fresh spinach should have dark green leaves that are crisp and free of moisture and mold. Avoid buying spinach with broken or bruised leaves. Rinse fresh spinach thoroughly in cold water to remove any sand; pat dry and refrigerate in a plastic bag lined with a paper towel up to 3 days.

Nutrition Analysis (*Per Serving*): Calories: 190 / Cholesterol: 14 mg / Carbohydrates: 12 g / Protein: 3 g / Sodium: 121 mg / Fat: 16 g (Saturated Fat: 4 g) / Potassium: 289 mg.

STUFFED ARTICHOKES

Makes 2 Servings

- 2 medium artichokes
- 1 tablespoon lemon juice
- ½ cup finely chopped fresh mushrooms
- 2 small cloves garlic, minced
- 3 tablespoons olive oil
- 1 cup fine dry bread crumbs
- ¼ cup finely chopped pimiento-stuffed green olives
- ¼ cup snipped fresh parsley
- ¼ cup grated Parmesan cheese
- ¼ teaspoon pepper

♦   ♦   ♦

The White Crane Wellness Center is a nonprofit senior center, focusing on achieving good health through exercise and eating well. One method of reaching this goal is through cooking classes. During classes, students either split into groups and each group prepares a dish, or a nutritionist prepares and presents dishes. It was from these classes that the idea for <u>Growing Older, Eating Better</u> emerged. The cookbook includes recipes from the class and some favorite recipes from the seniors.

<u>Growing Older, Eating Better</u>
The White Crane
Wellness Center
Chicago
ILLINOIS

1 Remove the stems and loose outer leaves from the artichokes. Cut off 1 inch from the tops and snip off the sharp leaf tips. Brush the cut edges with a little lemon juice.

2 In a large covered saucepan or Dutch oven, cook the artichokes in boiling, *salted water* for 20 to 30 minutes or until a leaf pulls out easily. Remove the artichokes from the saucepan and drain them upside down.

3 Remove the center leaves and the fuzzy "choke."

4 Meanwhile, in a medium skillet, cook the mushrooms and garlic in the oil. Cook and stir until the mushrooms are tender. Remove from heat; stir in the bread crumbs, olives, parsley, Parmesan cheese and pepper.

5 Preheat the oven to 375°. Spoon the mixture into the centers and in between the leaves of the artichokes.

6 Place the stuffed artichokes in a 9x9x2-inch baking pan, making sure the artichokes won't tip over. Cover and bake in the 375° oven for 15 minutes. Uncover and bake about 10 minutes more or until the artichokes are heated through.

 TIPS FROM OUR KITCHEN

When shopping for artichokes, look for compact, firm globes that are heavy for their size. Summer and fall artichokes will be more conical with slightly flared leaves. Avoid artichokes with mottled or spread leaves or shriveled cones. Leaf edges may be darkened because of chill damage but this doesn't affect the quality.

Store fresh artichokes in a plastic bag in the refrigerator up to 1 week, but for the best quality use within a couple days.

Nutrition Analysis (*Per Serving*): Calories: 525 / Cholesterol: 10 mg / Carbohydrates: 53 g / Protein: 17 g / Sodium: 1161 mg / Fat: 29 g (Saturated Fat: 6 g) / Potassium: 652 mg.

STUFFED ARTICHOKES

side

salads

Instead of plain rice or vegetables, try one of these creative side salads and turn dinner from something good into something great. Combining zesty flavor with a striking presentation, Green Rice Ring is perfect for a special evening with family or friends. For a surprising take on an old favorite, you'll enjoy Sweet Potato Salad with its hints of ginger and orange. And Braised Belgian Endive, Snow Pea Splendor, and Broccoli Salad are all palate-pleasing ways to "eat your veggies!"

RED, WHITE AND BLUE GELATIN MOLD

RED, WHITE AND BLUE GELATIN MOLD

Makes 12 Servings

- 1 6-ounce package strawberry-flavored gelatin
- 1 10-ounce package frozen strawberries
- 1 8-ounce package cream cheese, softened
- 1 8-ounce carton dairy sour cream
- ¾ cup salad dressing *or* mayonnaise
- 1 tablespoon lemon juice
- 1 envelope unflavored gelatin
- 1 6-ounce package blackberry-flavored gelatin
- 2 cups frozen blueberries

◆ ◆ ◆

The Immanuel Lutheran Church Cookbook was created to raise funds for a scholarship program for the Valparaiso University. Recipes were submitted by members of the congregation. Fern Niemann contributed this recipe for Red, White and Blue Gelatin Mold, which she says is "a perfect dish for a Fourth of July picnic."

Fern Niemann
Immanuel Lutheran Church Cookbook
Immanuel Lutheran Ladies Aid
Immanuel Lutheran Church
Michigan City
INDIANA

1 Lightly oil an 11- to 12-cup mold; set aside.

2 Pour 2 cups *boiling water* over the strawberry-flavored gelatin; stir until the gelatin is dissolved. Carefully stir in the frozen strawberries. Chill until the mixture begins to thicken. Stir to distribute the strawberries evenly and turn the mixture into the prepared mold. Refrigerate.

3 In a small bowl, beat the cream cheese, sour cream, salad dressing or mayonnaise and lemon juice with an electric mixer until the mixture is smooth.

4 In a small custard cup, sprinkle the unflavored gelatin into ¼ cup *cold water*. Place the custard cup in a skillet with ½ inch of boiling water. Stir the gelatin over the *boiling water* until the gelatin is dissolved. Stir the unflavored gelatin mixture into the cream cheese mixture. Beat until well blended. Carefully spoon the gelatin-cream cheese mixture over the strawberry mixture. Spread the gelatin-cream cheese mixture evenly to the edge of the mold. Refrigerate.

5 Pour 2 cups *boiling water* over the blackberry-flavored gelatin and stir until the gelatin is thoroughly dissolved. Add ½ cup *cold water* and the frozen blueberries; stir. Chill until the mixture begins to thicken. Stir again to distribute the blueberries. Spoon the mixture over the cream cheese layer in the mold and spread evenly to the edge of the mold.

6 Refrigerate the gelatin mold until it is firm, preferably overnight. Unmold onto a serving dish.

TIPS FROM OUR KITCHEN

To quick-chill gelatin, place the bowl of gelatin mixture over a bowl of ice water; stir until partially set.

The trick to a successful layered gelatin salad is knowing when to add the next layer. If the first layer is chilled too long, the second layer won't adhere; if it's not chilled long enough, the layers run together. The correct time to add the second layer is when the first layer appears firm but is slightly sticky to the touch. At this stage the gelatin will retain a fingerprint.

To unmold a gelatin salad, first, loosen the edges of the gelatin mixture from the sides of the mold with the tip of a sharp knife or thin metal spatula. Second, dip the mold into warm (*not hot*) water to the depth of the gelatin contents. Hold about 5 seconds. Tilt or shake the mold gently to loosen. Third, invert the serving plate on top of the mold. Hold both together firmly and invert. Fourth, shake the mold gently until the gelatin slips from the mold onto the serving dish or plate. If the gelatin doesn't release, repeat the process.

Nutrition Analysis (*Per Serving*): Calories: 250 / Cholesterol: 33 mg / Carbohydrates: 26 g / Protein: 4 g / Sodium: 182 mg / Fat: 16 g (Saturated Fat: 7 g) / Potassium: 105 mg.

GREEN RICE RING

Makes 18 Side-Dish Servings
- 6 cups hot cooked rice
- 2 cups shredded Monterey Jack *or* cheddar cheese (8 ounces)
- 1 4-ounce can chopped green chilies
- ½ to 1 teaspoon pepper
- 1 16-ounce carton dairy sour cream
- 1 pimiento, cut into strips

Celery leaves (optional)
Tomato wedges (optional)
Shredded lettuce (optional)

◆　　◆　　◆

When St. Albert the Great Newman Center & Parish members needed to raise funds, they put together a cookbook with the help of Maggie Gamboa, a local restaurateur and caterer. During her thirty years in the business, Maggie's clients have included the U.S. Congress, the U.S. Treasurer's office and a movie production company. We are delighted to have this opportunity to try one of Maggie's wonderful dishes, Green Rice Ring.

Maggie Gamboa
Recetas Del Valle
St. Albert the Great Newman Center & Parish
Las Cruces
NEW MEXICO

1 Preheat the oven to 350°. Grease an 8-cup ring mold. Set aside.

2 In a large bowl, combine the rice, cheese, chilies and pepper. Toss to mix well. Stir in the sour cream.

3 Spoon the cheese mixture into the prepared 8-cup ring mold, packing lightly with the back of a spoon. Bake in the 350° oven for 30 minutes. Cool the rice ring in the mold on a wire rack for 5 minutes.

4 Loosen the edges with a knife. To unmold onto a serving plate, cover the top of the mold with the serving plate, invert both and lift off the mold. Place pimiento strips over the top of the ring. If desired, fill the center with celery leaves and tomato wedges and frame the base of the ring with shredded lettuce.

 TIPS FROM OUR KITCHEN

To make 6 cups cooked rice, start with 2 cups raw long grain rice or 3 cups raw quick-cooking rice. Follow package directions for cooking and add 1 teaspoon salt.

Nutrition Analysis *(Per Serving)*: Calories: 287 / Cholesterol: 34 mg / Carbohydrates: 31 g / Protein: 9 g / Sodium: 167 mg / Fat: 14 g (Saturated Fat: 9 g) / Potassium: 118 mg.

GREEN RICE RING

SNOW PEA SPLENDOR

SNOW PEA SPLENDOR

Makes 8 Servings
- ¼ cup sesame seed
- ½ cup salad oil
- 2 tablespoons lemon juice
- 2 tablespoons vinegar
- 2 tablespoons sugar
- 1 clove garlic, crushed
- ½ teaspoon salt
- 1 pound fresh pea pods
- 4 slices bacon
- 4 cups shredded lettuce
- ½ cup snipped parsley

◆   ◆   ◆

For a time, Faye Bullock and her husband ran a lodge in western United States. There, she gained a reputation as an innovative and inspiring cook who loved to try new things. We're sure you'll be inspired by her Snow Pea Splendor.

Faye Bullock
Paths of Sunshine
Florida Federations of
Garden Clubs, Inc.
Winter Park
FLORIDA

1 To toast the sesame seed, spread them in a thin layer in a shallow ungreased baking pan. Bake in a 350° oven for 10 to 15 minutes or until golden, stirring once or twice. In a glass jar with a tight-fitting lid, combine the toasted sesame seed, salad oil, lemon juice, vinegar, sugar, garlic and salt. Cover and refrigerate.

2 Remove the stems from the pea pods. Steam 30 seconds. Cover and chill.

3 Fry the bacon until crisp. Drain on paper towels, then crumble.

4 In a large salad bowl, toss the lettuce, parsley, pea pods and bacon. Shake the dressing until well blended. Pour the desired amount of dressing over the salad; toss. Serve immediately.

 TIPS FROM OUR KITCHEN

If you have leftover dressing, store it in the refrigerator to use another day. It makes a delicious dressing for spinach salad or cooked green beans.

To make carrot cutouts, thinly slice a large carrot. Use a small canape cutter to make flower shapes.

Nutrition Analysis (*Per Serving*): Calories: 205 / Cholesterol: 3 mg / Carbohydrates: 10 g / Protein: 4 g / Sodium: 191 mg / Fat: 17 g (Saturated Fat: 3 g) / Potassium: 225 mg.

SWEET POTATO SALAD

Makes 12 Servings

- 3 pounds sweet potatoes, peeled and cut into ½-inch cubes
- ¼ teaspoon salt
- 1½ cups dairy sour cream
- ⅔ cup mayonnaise
- 2 tablespoons chopped crystallized ginger
- 2 teaspoons grated orange peel
- 1 20-ounce can crushed pineapple, well drained
- 4 stalks celery, sliced
- 1 cup walnut halves
- 1 cup raisins

✦ ✦ ✦

This pretty, colorful dish often becomes a conversation piece when Elise Dolgow serves it at summer barbecues. Elise says that she likes to serve dishes that are "different" to her guests. She says that folks are surprised and delighted by this unusual twist on an old favorite.

Elise Dolgow
Chef's EscORT
Women's American Organization for Rehabilitation Through Training, Inc., Southeast District
Parkland
FLORIDA

1 In a large saucepan, place the sweet potatoes, salt and enough water to cover. Bring the water to boiling; reduce heat and simmer for 10 to 15 minutes or just until sweet potatoes are tender. Drain and cool.

2 In a small mixing bowl, stir together the sour cream, mayonnaise, ginger and orange peel. Beat until creamy.

3 In a very large mixing bowl, carefully fold together the cooled potatoes, pineapple, celery, walnuts and raisins.

4 Gradually add the mayonnaise mixture to the potato mixture, tossing lightly to avoid mashing the potatoes. Cover and chill for 12 to 24 hours. Serve cold.

TIPS FROM OUR KITCHEN

To cube the sweet potatoes easily, first use a chef's knife to cut the potato into ½-inch strips, then cut crosswise to make cubes.

If you prefer a creamier potato salad, stir in 1 to 2 tablespoons *milk* to the already dressed salad.

If desired, save the celery leaves for a garnish.

For a festive presentation, serve the salad on a lettuce leaf.

Nutrition Analysis (*Per Serving*): Calories: 372 / Cholesterol: 20 mg / Carbohydrates: 42 g / Protein: 5 g / Sodium: 154 mg / Fat: 22 g (Saturated Fat: 6 g) Potassium: 579 mg.

SWEET POTATO SALAD

PERFECT POTATO SALAD

PERFECT POTATO SALAD

6 medium potatoes
   (2 pounds), unpeeled
½ cup mayonnaise
¼ cup milk
2 teaspoons cider vinegar
2 teaspoons minced onion
1 to 2 teaspoons prepared
   mustard
½ teaspoon salt
⅛ teaspoon coarsely ground
   black pepper
2 medium celery stalks,
   thinly sliced (1 cup)
Lettuce leaves

♦   ♦   ♦

*Sonia Dohrmann contributed
this recipe to the Angel Food
cookbook because it's an easy
recipe that she thought many
others would be able to use. Sonia
said that she takes Perfect Potato
Salad to barbecues and picnics,
and that one of the reasons she
likes it is because it can be doubled
so easily.*

Sonia Dohrmann
Angel Food
The Women's Minis-tree of the
Roxborough Presbyterian Church
Philadelphia
PENNSYLVANIA

1 In a 4-quart saucepan, place the un-peeled potatoes in enough *water* to cover. Bring the water to a boil over high heat. Reduce heat to medium-low; cover and cook for 25 to 30 minutes or until the potatoes are tender.

2 Drain the potatoes and let them stand until cool enough to handle. Peel the cooled potatoes and cut them into bite-size chunks.

3 In a large bowl, stir together the mayonnaise, milk, cider vinegar, onion, mustard, salt and pepper; mix well.

4 Add the potatoes and celery to the mayonnaise mixture; toss gently to coat.

5 Line a serving bowl or platter with lettuce leaves. Spoon the potato salad on top of the lettuce leaves and serve.

TIPS FROM OUR KITCHEN

White and red potatoes are the best choice for this salad because they hold their shape and texture after cooking. Russet potatoes, however, have a mealy, dry texture, which is more suited to baking and frying.

For faster cooking, cut the unpeeled potatoes into quarters before boiling them.

Cider vinegar is made from apple juice. It is less sharp in flavor than distilled or white vinegar. For a different taste, you can substitute an herb flavored vinegar in this recipe.

Serve this salad immediately after making, or prepare it ahead of time and keep it in the refrigerator until you are ready to serve.

Nutrition Analysis (*Per Serving*): Calories: 272 / Cholesterol: 11 mg / Carbohydrates: 32 g / Protein: 3 g / Sodium: 319 mg / Fat: 15 g (Saturated Fat: 3 g) / Potassium: 588 mg.

CARROT SALAD

Makes 8 to 10 Servings

2 pounds carrots, thinly sliced (about 6 cups)
2 medium onions, thinly sliced and separated into rings
1 green sweet pepper, sliced into thin strips
Marinade:
1 10¾-ounce can condensed tomato soup
¾ cup vinegar
⅔ cup sugar
⅓ cup cooking oil
1 teaspoon Worcestershire sauce
1 teaspoon prepared mustard
¼ teaspoon salt

◆ ◆ ◆

Jean Farinacci has the recipe for Carrot Salad (also called Copper Pennies) tucked away in her files and occasionally she uses it for "salad suppers for a different and interesting tangy taste." She recommends that the salad accompany roast beef.

Jean Farinacci
The Market Basket
Witan
Akron
OHIO

1 In a large saucepan, cook the carrots in a small amount of *water* about 8 minutes or just until tender. Remove from heat; drain.

2 In a large mixing bowl or salad bowl, stir together the cooked carrots, onions and green sweet pepper; set aside.

3 To make the marinade: In a medium bowl, stir together the undiluted tomato soup, vinegar, sugar, cooking oil, Worcestershire sauce, mustard and salt.

4 Pour the marinade over the vegetables. Stir to coat the vegetables with the marinade. Cover and refrigerate for 4 hours or overnight, stirring occasionally. Drain and discard the marinade before serving.

 TIPS FROM OUR KITCHEN

Two pounds of carrots will yield about 6 cups of ¼-inch-thick slices. For faster slicing, use your food processor.

If desired, substitute yellow sweet pepper for half or all of the green sweet pepper in this recipe.

Either cider vinegar or white vinegar can be used in this recipe. You might also want to experiment with flavored vinegars, such as basil or garlic vinegar.

For party serving, chop the green sweet pepper and onion instead of slicing them. Then, serve the salad in halved and seeded green or yellow sweet peppers.

Nutrition Analysis (*Per Serving*): Calories: 107 / Cholesterol: 0 mg / Carbohydrates: 19 g / Protein: 2 g / Sodium: 143 mg / Fat: 3 g (Saturated Fat: 1 g) / Potassium: 315 mg.

CARROT SALAD

MARINATED COLESLAW

MARINATED COLESLAW

Makes 10 to 12 Servings

6 to 8	cups shredded cabbage
1	cup shredded carrot
½	cup chopped green sweet pepper (optional)
¼ to ⅓	cup sugar
½	teaspoon unflavored gelatin
¼	cup cider vinegar
2	tablespoons cold water
⅓	cup salad oil
1	teaspoon celery seed
¼	teaspoon salt
⅛	teaspoon pepper
¼	cup dairy sour cream

♦ ♦ ♦

Lorraine Stumbo and two of her neighbors had an annual Christmas cookie baking session during which they would bake, eat and "solve all the problems of the world." While they were baking, eating and solving, they were also sharing recipes. It was during one of the sessions, about ten years ago, that Lorraine was given the recipe for Marinated Coleslaw. Lorraine tells us that this salad is a great way for her to use up her garden's bounty.

Lorraine Stumbo
<u>*Country Collection*</u>
Bethel Church
Ogden
IOWA

1 In a large bowl, toss together the cabbage, carrot and, if desired, chopped pepper. Set aside.

2 In a small saucepan, stir together the sugar and gelatin. Add the vinegar and water. Bring to a boil, stirring constantly. Remove from heat and cool.

3 Pour the cooled dressing into a blender container. Add the salad oil, celery seed, salt and pepper; cover and blend well. Add the sour cream and blend just until combined.

4 Pour the dressing over the vegetables and toss to coat. Before serving, cover and refrigerate for several hours or overnight.

 TIPS FROM OUR KITCHEN

For a more colorful salad, try using a mixture of red and green cabbage and/or red, green and yellow sweet pepper.

There is no need to soften the gelatin in this recipe because mixing it with the sugar will ensure that the gelatin will not clump when the water is added.

This coleslaw is a perfect dish to take along on a picnic, but make sure that you keep it on ice in your cooler so that it doesn't spoil.

Nutrition Analysis *(Per Serving)*: Calories: 113 / Cholesterol: 3 mg / Carbohydrates: 10 g / Protein: 1 g / Sodium: 71 mg / Fat: 9 g (Saturated Fat: 2 g) / Potassium: 190 mg.

BRAISED BELGIAN ENDIVE

Makes 8 Servings
4 heads Belgian endive
2 tablespoons butter *or* margarine
2 tablespoons chicken broth
2 to 4 teaspoons lemon juice
½ teaspoon sugar
½ teaspoon salt
⅛ teaspoon pepper
Paprika *and/or* snipped fresh parsley

♦   ♦   ♦

This recipe is a simplified version of Mary Hill Caperton's cousin's recipe for Braised Belgian Endive. Mary says that she usually includes both the parsley and the paprika and suggests trying vermouth or white wine in place of the chicken stock for a flavor variation.

Mary Hill Caperton
SPCA Cookbook
Abermale SPCA
Charlottesville
VIRGINIA

1 Preheat the oven to 350°.

2 Wash and drain the endive heads. Halve the endive lengthwise; cut out and discard the cores. Place the endive in a 2-quart rectangular baking dish.

3 In a small saucepan, melt the butter or margarine. Stir in the chicken broth, lemon juice, sugar, salt and pepper. Pour the mixture over the endive.

4 Cover and bake in the 350° oven for 35 to 40 minutes or until the endive is tender.

5 Using a slotted spoon, transfer the endive to a warm serving dish. Sprinkle with paprika and/or parsley.

TIPS FROM OUR KITCHEN

Belgian endive also is known as French endive or witloof chicory. The individual heads are small and cone-shaped with 5- to 6-inch-long, tightly packed leaves that are creamy white with pale yellow tips. The flavor is slightly bitter. After purchasing, store endive in a plastic bag in the refrigerator up to 3 days. Since it is usually imported, Belgian endive can be expensive, but the delicious vegetable makes a perfect company dish.

One medium lemon will yield approximately 3 tablespoons fresh lemon juice. You can store leftover lemon juice in the refrigerator for 2 to 3 days.

For variety, sprinkle the baked endive with 2 tablespoons chopped, toasted pecans or almonds in the place of the paprika and/or parsley.

You can make the chicken broth using instant chicken bouillon granules and water. Or, use canned broth or homemade, if you have it on hand.

To braise is to cook food slowly in a small amount of liquid in a tightly covered pan.

Nutrition Analysis (*Per Serving*): Calories: 32 / Cholesterol: 8 mg / Carbohydrates: 1 g / Protein: 0 g / Sodium: 176 mg / Fat: 3 g (Saturated Fat: 2 g) / Potassium: 58 mg.

BRAISED BELGIAN ENDIVE

GREEN BEAN AND PARMESAN CHEESE SALAD

GREEN BEAN AND PARMESAN CHEESE SALAD

Makes 8 Servings

2¼ pounds fresh green beans, ends trimmed
⅓ cup olive oil
⅓ cup white wine vinegar
2 cloves garlic, minced
⅛ teaspoon freshly ground pepper
1 cup pecans, chopped and toasted
¾ cup coarsely grated imported Parmesan cheese
Freshly ground pepper (optional)

♦   ♦   ♦

Because Carole Carney Creamer and her family are very "vegetable-oriented" and are strong believers that garlic is very good for your health, Green Bean and Parmesan Cheese Salad is the perfect dish for them. Carole told us that all of her cooking is healthy cooking, and this nutritious salad is no exception.

Carole Carney Creamer
The Dollar-A-Month Club
Anniversary Cookbook: A Collection of Recipes to Celebrate the Year
The Jesuit Jamshedpur Mission
Baltimore
MARYLAND

1 Place the green beans in a steamer with a steamer basket or in a large saucepan with a colander set over *boiling water.* Cover the steamer or saucepan and steam the green beans about 10 minutes or until barely crisp-tender. Drain the green beans; set aside.

2 Meanwhile, in a screw-top jar, combine the olive oil, white wine vinegar, garlic and pepper. Cover the jar and shake well to blend the ingredients.

3 Place the drained green beans in a large bowl. Pour the dressing over the beans. Let the beans stand for 10 minutes, stirring once or twice.

4 If the beans will not be served after the standing time, refrigerate them. Let the beans return to room temperature before serving. Just before serving, sprinkle the green beans with the toasted pecans and Parmesan cheese. If desired, serve with the additional freshly ground pepper.

 TIPS FROM OUR KITCHEN

Wash fresh green beans and refrigerate them in an airtight plastic bag for 3 to 4 days.

In this recipe, you steam the green beans in the vapors from the boiling water, not in the water itself, to retain flavor, color and vitamins. If you don't have a steamer, use a colander set in a covered saucepan; the water level should not touch the bottom of the colander.

Because the Parmesan cheese is so important to the flavor of this salad, be sure to taste a variety of mild to robust types in order to select the one that you prefer.

Nutrition Analysis (*Per Serving*): Calories: 256 / Cholesterol: 7 mg / Carbohydrates: 14 g / Protein: 8 g / Sodium: 124 mg / Fat: 21 g (Saturated Fat: 2 g) / Potassium: 440 mg.

FOUR BEAN SALAD

✦   ✦   ✦

Dee Daniels says she discovered this great recipe about twenty-seven years ago when she was living in California.

Dee Daniels
<u>**There's More to Lima than Beans**</u>
The Lima and Allen County
Medical Alliance
Lima
OHIO

1 Cut the green sweet pepper and onion rings in half, reserving *2* whole pepper rings for a garnish.

2 In a large bowl, stir together the drained green beans, yellow wax beans, garbanzo beans, red kidney beans, the green sweet pepper ring halves and the onion ring halves.

3 To make the dressing: In a glass jar with a tight fitting lid, combine the wine vinegar, salad oil, sugar, parsley, dry mustard, basil, tarragon and salt. Cover and shake to blend the ingredients.

4 Drizzle the dressing over the bean mixture. Cover and refrigerate the salad for several hours or overnight, stirring once or twice.

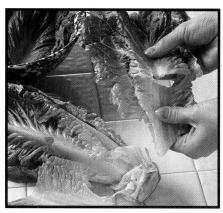

5 Remove the bottom stems from the romaine leaves. Line a salad bowl with the romaine; set aside.

6 Before serving, stir the salad again; drain.

7 To serve, spoon the drained bean salad into the romaine-lined bowl. Garnish with the reserved green sweet pepper rings.

 TIPS FROM OUR KITCHEN

For a change of pace, you can use frozen Italian beans that have been cooked and drained or canned black beans that have been drained and rinsed in place of one of the beans in this recipe. As another variation, add canned whole kernel corn that has been drained to the salad.

Rinsing canned beans helps to remove some of the salt added during the canning process.

In place of the romaine, you can use leaf lettuce, butterhead, spinach or red cabbage to line the salad bowl.

Nutrition Analysis (*Per Serving*): Calories: 203 / Cholesterol: 0 mg / Carbohydrates: 27 g / Protein: 4 g / Sodium: 330 mg / Fat: 10 g (Saturated Fat: 1 g) / Potassium: 322 mg.

FOUR BEAN SALAD

CAULIFLOWER SALAD

CAULIFLOWER SALAD

Makes 6 Servings

1	pound cauliflower, broken into flowerets and thinly sliced into bite-size pieces (4 cups)
1	cup thinly sliced radishes
1	bunch green onions, thinly sliced (½ cup)
½	cup sliced, pitted ripe olives
½	cup chopped watercress
1	8-ounce carton dairy sour cream
1½	tablespoons lemon juice
1	tablespoon grated Parmesan cheese
1	clove garlic, minced
¼	teaspoon salt
⅛	teaspoon pepper
Dash ground red pepper	

♦   ♦   ♦

When Barbara Lewis lived in California, she and her husband attended a potluck Christmas party, where she tasted a fellow party goer's Cauliflower Salad. Barbara asked for the recipe. Now, when the Ladies of the Ribbon have their two annual cookouts, this is the dish Barbara brings every time!

Barbara Lewis
Pot Luck From Ladies
of the Ribbon
Ladies of the Ribbon
Bradenton
FLORIDA

1 In a large bowl, combine the cauliflower, radishes, onions, olives and watercress. Toss gently and set aside.

2 In a blender container, combine the sour cream, lemon juice, Parmesan cheese, garlic, salt, pepper and red pepper. Cover and blend well.

3 Pour the dressing over the vegetables, tossing to coat. Cover and refrigerate up to 2 hours.

 TIPS FROM OUR KITCHEN

To prepare fresh cauliflower: Rinse the entire head under cold water. Remove and discard the outer green leaves. Using a knife, remove and discard the woody stem. Break or cut the flowerets from the head.

If desired, you can use broccoli for all or part of the cauliflower in this recipe. If watercress isn't available, substitute finely snipped spinach.

The leaves and stems of watercress, while delicate in appearance, have a lively, peppery tang. When shopping, choose watercress with healthy-looking stems and bright green leaves. Clean watercress by dunking it in a large bowl of cold water. Repeat with fresh water until no more sand or dirt collects in the bowl. Pat dry. Store in a plastic bag with a paper towel.

This salad can be made up to 24 hours before serving. If you plan to do so, however, wait to add the watercress until just before serving since it has a tendency to release water into the salad.

Light sour cream can be used instead of regular sour cream.

Garnish the salad with radish roses or radish accordions and additional watercress. Or, try garnishing with a green onion brush. To make an onion brush, use just the green portion of green onion and make slashes at both ends of the onion to make fringes. Place in ice water to curl the ends.

Nutrition Analysis (*Per Serving*): Calories: 124 / Cholesterol: 18 mg / Carbohydrates: 7 g / Protein: 4 g / Sodium: 197 mg / Fat: 10 g (Saturated Fat: 5 g) / Potassium: 387 mg.

Broccoli Salad

6 cups chopped fresh broccoli *or* loose-pack frozen cut broccoli (1½ sixteen-ounce bags)

8 slices bacon, cooked crisp, drained and crumbled

1 cup pecan pieces

½ cup raisins

½ medium red onion, chopped

¾ cup salad dressing *or* mayonnaise

2 tablespoons sugar

2 tablespoons vinegar

♦ ♦ ♦

Jan Wozniak's daughter gave her this recipe six or seven years ago. Jan changed the recipe slightly and now she cooks the broccoli al dente and uses turkey bacon. She often takes her Broccoli Salad to holiday brunches. Jan said that everyone always comments on how good the salad tastes, and she thinks it's because the pecans add extra flavor.

Jan Wozniak
Immanuel Lutheran Church
Cookbook
Immanuel Lutheran Ladies Aid
Immanuel Lutheran Church
Michigan City
INDIANA

1 In a large saucepan, cook the broccoli in a small amount of lightly salted *boiling water* for 5 to 7 minutes or until the broccoli is crisp-tender. Drain the broccoli; let cool.

2 In a large bowl, combine the cooled broccoli, crumbled bacon, pecans, raisins and red onion.

3 In a small bowl, stir together the salad dressing or mayonnaise, sugar and vinegar until well mixed.

4 Pour the dressing over the broccoli mixture; toss to coat the vegetables with the dressing. Cover and chill the salad for 2 to 24 hours. Stir the salad before serving.

 TIPS FROM OUR KITCHEN

You'll need 2 to 3 stalks of broccoli (about 1 pound) to yield the 6 cups of chopped broccoli called for in this recipe. Remove the outer leaves and trim and discard the tough portions of the stems.

For a brighter green color, steam the broccoli for 8 to 12 minutes. If you don't have a steamer, use a wire mesh strainer or basket positioned above boiling water in a Dutch oven. To prevent overcooking, transfer crisp-tender cooked broccoli to a strainer or colander and rinse under cold running water.

Another cooking option for the broccoli is the microwave. Place the broccoli in a microwave-safe dish. Add 2 tablespoons water and cover the dish; micro-cook on 100% power (high) for 4 to 7 minutes or until the broccoli is crisp-tender, stirring once.

Quick to cook, bacon can be baked or micro-cooked.
 To bake: Place the slices on a rack in a shallow baking pan. Bake, uncovered, in a 400° oven for 15 to 18 minutes.
 To micro-cook: Place the slices on a microwave-safe rack or paper plate. Cover with microwave-safe paper towels. Micro-cook 4 slices on 100% power (high) for 2½ to 3½ minutes.

If desired, you can substitute 1 cup of cubed cooked ham for the bacon in this recipe.

No-fat or reduced-fat mayonnaise or salad dressing can be used in this recipe.

Nutrition Analysis (*Per Serving*): Calories: 277 / Cholesterol: 11 mg / Carbohydrates: 23 g / Protein: 6 g / Sodium: 281 mg / Fat: 20 g (Saturated Fat: 3 g) / Potassium: 413 mg.

BROCCOLI SALAD

chapter six

main course
salads

Salads no longer linger on the sidelines of appetizing eating, but proudly have come to the center stage of American meals. Main course salads are particularly marvelous because they can fill you up, satisfy your tastebuds, and fulfill most of your nutritional needs—all at the same time! Either colorful Cobb Salad or sophisticated Salad Niçoise can be the eye-catching star of a summertime spread. For the pasta lover, Hemenway's Seafood Pasta Salad and Italian Pasta Salad are both molto bene. And, Hot Chicken Salad is just what the doctor ordered to beat the Monday night dinner blues.

COBB SALAD

COBB SALAD

Makes 6 Servings

Dressing:

- ⅔ cup salad oil
- ⅓ cup white wine vinegar
- 1 clove garlic, split
- ½ teaspoon Worcestershire sauce
- ½ teaspoon dry mustard
- ½ teaspoon paprika
- ½ teaspoon sugar
- ½ teaspoon salt
- ¼ teaspoon pepper

Salad:

- 8 cups torn iceberg lettuce
- 2½ cups torn chicory
- 1½ cups torn watercress
- 1¾ cups chopped tomatoes
- 2½ cups cooked, cubed, white meat chicken
- 6 slices bacon, cooked and crumbled
- 2 hard-cooked eggs, finely diced
- ⅔ cup crumbled blue cheese
- 2 cups diced green sweet pepper *and/or* avocado
- 2 tablespoons snipped fresh chives

♦   ♦   ♦

Since its founding in 1926, the women of The Junior League of Pasadena have logged countless hours of community service. California Heritage Cookbook is a major fund-raiser that helps to support their worthy efforts.

California Heritage Cookbook
The Junior League of Pasadena
Pasadena
CALIFORNIA

1 To make the dressing: Combine the oil, vinegar, garlic, Worcestershire sauce, dry mustard, paprika, sugar, salt and pepper in a jar with a tight-fitting lid. Shake the jar vigorously to blend the ingredients. Refrigerate the dressing.

2 Toss the lettuce with the chicory and watercress. Line a large platter or shallow bowl with the mixed greens.

3 Arrange the tomatoes, chicken, bacon, eggs, blue cheese and sweet pepper and/or avocado in bands across the layer of greens.

4 Just before serving the salad, shake the jar of dressing well, then remove the garlic.

5 Present the arranged salad to your guests, then pour just enough dressing over it to moisten the ingredients. Next, toss the salad and sprinkle it with the chives.

 TIPS FROM OUR KITCHEN

If you can't find chicory in your area, escarole or radicchio are "kissin' cousins." Either one will add just the right amount of pleasantly bitter tang to this salad.

Nutrition Analysis (*Per Serving*): Calories: 511 / Cholesterol: 140 mg / Carbohydrates: 15 g / Protein: 29 g / Sodium: 650 mg / Fat: 39 g (Saturated Fat: 9 g) / Potassium: 1,230 mg.

HOT CHICKEN SALAD

Makes 8 Servings

- 4 cups cold, chopped cooked chicken
- 4 hard-cooked eggs, chopped
- 1 10¾-ounce can condensed cream of chicken *or* cream of celery soup
- 1 cup chopped celery
- ¾ cup mayonnaise *or* salad dressing
- 2 pimientos, chopped (½ cup)
- 2 tablespoons lemon juice
- 1 teaspoon finely chopped onion
- 1 cup shredded cheddar cheese (4 ounces)
- 1½ cups crushed potato chips (3 cups whole chips)
- ⅔ cup slivered almonds

❖   ❖   ❖

Dolores Ruth's daughter, Dottie Ruth Arnold, gave her this recipe for Hot Chicken Salad. Dottie recommends serving this salad with French or crispy rolls and fresh fruit. She also said that it travels well to potluck dinners.

Dolores E. Ruth
*The Dollar-A-Month Club
Anniversary Cookbook: A
Collection of Recipes to Celebrate
the Year*
The Jesuit Jamshedpur Mission
Baltimore
MARYLAND

1 Grease a 2-quart oval or rectangular baking dish; set aside.

2 In a large bowl, toss together the chopped chicken, eggs, undiluted cream of chicken or cream of celery soups, chopped celery, mayonnaise or salad dressing, pimientos, lemon juice and onion.

3 Spoon the chicken mixture into the prepared baking dish. Sprinkle with the cheddar cheese.

4 In a small bowl, stir together the crushed potato chips and slivered almonds. Sprinkle the mixture over the chicken salad. Cover and refrigerate overnight.

5 Preheat the oven to 400°. Bake, uncovered, about 30 minutes or until heated through. Cover the top loosely with aluminum foil, if necessary, to prevent overbrowning.

 TIPS FROM OUR KITCHEN

You can use frozen, chopped cooked chicken or cook your own fresh chicken for this recipe. Use 4 whole medium *chicken breasts* (about 3 pounds), halved and skinned, or 1½ pounds skinned and boned *chicken breast halves*. Place the chicken in a Dutch oven with 1⅓ cups *water*. Bring the mixture to a boil; reduce heat. Cover and simmer for 18 to 20 minutes for bone-in chicken or for 12 to 14 minutes for boneless pieces, or until the chicken is tender and no longer pink. Drain the chicken, cool and cut it into cubes.

To crush potato chips, place the whole chips in a heavy plastic bag and use a rolling pin or press with your fingers to crush them to the desired size. Mixing the chips with the almonds helps to prevent the almonds from getting too brown in the oven.

If desired, serve Hot Chicken Salad with pita wedges. Split 2 pita rounds in half horizontally. Cut each half into quarters to make 16 triangles. Place the triangles on a baking sheet. Bake in a 325° oven for 12 to 15 minutes or until the pita wedges are crisp.

Nutrition Analysis (*Per Serving*): Calories: 524 / Cholesterol: 199 mg / Carbohydrates: 13 g / Protein: 32 g / Sodium: 662 mg / Fat: 39 g (Saturated Fat: 10 g) / Potassium: 511 mg.

HOT CHICKEN SALAD

ITALIAN PASTA SALAD

Italian Pasta Salad

Makes 8 to 10 Servings

Salad:
- 8 ounces spiral pasta (rotini) cooked, drained and cooled
- 1 medium zucchini, sliced (1¼ cups)
- 1 medium green sweet pepper, chopped (¾ cup)
- 1 medium red sweet pepper, chopped (¾ cup)
- 1 tomato, seeded and chopped (⅔ cup)
- 3 ounces sliced pepperoni
- 2 ounces provolone cheese, cubed (½ cup)
- ½ cup snipped parsley
- ¼ cup chopped red onion
- 14 pitted ripe olives

Vinaigrette:
- ¼ cup balsamic vinegar
- 1 large clove garlic, minced
- 2 tablespoons vegetable oil
- 2 tablespoons olive oil
- 1 teaspoon dried basil, crushed, *or* 2 tablespoons snipped fresh basil
- ½ teaspoon salt
- ¼ teaspoon dried oregano, crushed, *or* 2 teaspoons snipped fresh oregano
- ¼ teaspoon freshly ground pepper

Fresh basil (optional)

◆　◆　◆

__Thyme & Monet Cookbook__

The Krasl Art Center

St. Joseph

MICHIGAN

1 To make the salad: In a large bowl, toss together the spiral pasta, zucchini, green sweet pepper, red sweet pepper, tomato, pepperoni, provolone cheese, parsley, red onion and olives.

2 To make the vinaigrette: In a small bowl, stir together the balsamic vinegar, garlic, vegetable oil, olive oil, basil, salt, oregano and pepper. Whisk the ingredients together until they are mixed. *Or,* add the vinaigrette ingredients to a jar with a tight-fitting lid and shake the jar vigorously to mix the ingredients.

3 Pour the vinaigrette over the salad and toss to coat the ingredients with the dressing. To let the flavors mellow, let the salad stand at room temperature for 30 minutes before serving. If desired, the salad may be made ahead and refrigerated. Let the salad stand for 30 minutes at room temperature before serving. Garnish with a sprig of fresh basil, if desired.

 TIPS FROM OUR KITCHEN

To seed a tomato easily, cut the tomato in half crosswise and use a spoon to remove the seeds.

If yellow sweet peppers are available, substitute 1 for part of the green sweet pepper to add even more color to the salad.

Rinsing the hot, cooked pasta with cold water helps to cool it quickly and prevents the pasta from sticking together. You may want to try rigatoni or mostaccioli instead of the rotini in this recipe.

There's a reason balsamic vinegar is more expensive than other varieties of vinegar: It's made from the juice of a very sweet white grape, then aged in wooden barrels for at least 10 years. The result is a vinegar dark brown in color with a delicate, sweet flavor.

Nutrition Analysis (*Per Serving*): Calories: 273 / Cholesterol: 13 mg / Carbohydrates: 27 g / Protein: 9 g / Sodium: 451 mg / Fat: 15 g (Saturated Fat: 4 g) / Potassium: 253 mg.

HEMENWAY'S SEAFOOD PASTA SALAD

Makes 5 Servings

- 6 ounces tri-colored rotini pasta (2½ cups)
- 12 ounces seafood including small peeled shrimp, lump crabmeat *and/or* cooked bay scallops
- 1 cup broccoli flowerets
- 1 tomato, chopped (¾ cup)
- 2 tablespoons finely chopped onion
- 2 tablespoons sliced pitted ripe olives

Dressing:
- ⅓ cup red wine vinegar
- ¼ cup olive oil
- 2 cloves garlic, minced
- ¼ teaspoon salt
- ¼ teaspoon sugar
- ¼ teaspoon dried thyme, crushed
- ¼ teaspoon dried oregano, crushed
- ¼ teaspoon dried basil, crushed
- 1 small bay leaf
- 2 to 3 cups mixed greens

◆　◆　◆

Hemenway's Restaurant submitted this recipe to the organization, Keep Providence Beautiful, to help in the effort to beautify Providence "through education and awareness."

Hemenway's Restaurant
<u>*Pasta Challenge*</u>
Keep Providence Beautiful
Providence
RHODE ISLAND

1 Cook the pasta according to the package directions. Drain and rinse with *cold water*. Drain again.

2 In a large bowl, toss together the shrimp, crabmeat and/or scallops with the cooked pasta. Add the broccoli, tomato, onion and olives; toss.

3 To make the dressing: In a screw-top jar, combine the vinegar, olive oil, garlic, salt, sugar, thyme, oregano, basil and bay leaf. Cover and shake well to combine.

4 Pour the dressing over the salad and toss to coat. Cover and refrigerate for 4 to 24 hours, stirring occasionally. Remove the bay leaf. Serve the pasta salad over the mixed greens.

 TIPS FROM OUR KITCHEN

To make broccoli flowerets, cut off the flower part from the stems and cut in half any flowers that are larger than bite size.

To cook fresh seafood: Bring a large saucepan of water to a boil. Add the shellfish and reduce heat to medium. Simmer the shrimp and/or scallops for 2 to 3 minutes or until the shrimp are pink and the scallops are opaque and firm. Simmer the fresh crabmeat for 25 minutes.

Rotini is also known as corkscrew pasta. In tri-colored pasta, a portion of the pasta is made in the usual manner, while some is flavored and colored with spinach and some with tomato.

When shopping for broccoli, look for firm stalks with deep green or purplish green, tightly packed heads. Store broccoli in a plastic bag in the refrigerator up to 4 days.

If fresh herbs are available, substitute ¾ teaspoon each for the dried thyme, oregano and basil in this recipe.

For a potluck or other large gathering this recipe can be doubled easily.

Nutrition Analysis (*Per Serving*): Calories: 324 / Cholesterol: 101 mg / Carbohydrates: 32 g / Protein: 20 g / Sodium: 303 mg / Fat: 13 g (Saturated Fat: 2 g) / Potassium: 390 mg.

HEMENWAY'S SEAFOOD PASTA SALAD

LAYERED SALAD

LAYERED SALAD

Makes 12 to 15 Servings

1 large head iceberg lettuce, torn into bite-size pieces (6 cups)

¼ teaspoon salt

⅛ teaspoon sugar

⅛ teaspoon pepper

6 hard-cooked eggs, sliced

1 10-ounce package frozen peas

½ pound bacon, cooked until crisp, drained and crumbled (10 slices)

2 cups shredded Swiss cheese (8 ounces)

1¼ to 1½ cups mayonnaise *or* salad dressing

1 to 3 green onions, sliced

Paprika

◆ ◆ ◆

Dolly Johnson, Director of Volunteer Services at Northwestern Memorial Hospital, told us about the projects that have benefited from the sales of <u>First There Must Be Food</u>. *One such project is bedside bingo. Through the use of closed-circuit television, patients are able to play bingo from their hospital beds.*

Food Services Department
<u>*First There Must Be Food*</u>
Northwestern Memorial Hospital
Chicago
ILLINOIS

1 Place *3 cups* of the lettuce in a salad bowl. Sprinkle with *⅛ teaspoon* of the salt, the sugar and the pepper.

2 Stand some egg slices decoratively against the side of the salad bowl. Cover the lettuce with the remaining egg slices. Sprinkle with the remaining salt.

3 Sprinkle the frozen peas over the eggs. Top with the remaining lettuce.

4 Sprinkle the bacon over the lettuce, and the shredded Swiss cheese over the bacon.

5 Carefully spread the mayonnaise or salad dressing evenly over the salad. Top with the green onions and sprinkle with paprika. Cover and chill for 2 to 24 hours. Toss the salad at the table before serving.

 TIPS FROM OUR KITCHEN

This salad will completely fill a 3-quart casserole. Therefore, you'll need at least a 4-quart bowl to allow room for tossing the salad.

To tailor this recipe to suit your own preferences, try substituting or adding shredded carrots, alfalfa sprouts, sweet green or red pepper, onion, broccoli or cauliflower. You might also vary the kind of cheese you use or include a layer of julienned ham or turkey. Instead of the iceberg lettuce, try red-tipped leaf lettuce or fresh spinach.

The easy way to produce perfect egg slices is to use an egg slicer, a gadget specifically designed for this purpose.

To crisp-cook this amount of bacon with no fuss or spatter, place the slices on a rack in a shallow baking pan. Bake, uncovered, in a 400° oven about 20 minutes or until crisp. Or, if you wish to use your microwave oven, place the bacon on a microwave-safe rack or a plate lined with paper towels. Cover with paper towels. Cook on 100% power (high) until done. Allow 4 to 5 minutes for 6 slices.

You can flavor the mayonnaise dressing with ½ teaspoon crushed dried tarragon or basil or 2 to 3 teaspoons lemon juice.

Nutrition Analysis (*Per Serving*): Calories: 324 / Cholesterol: 142 mg / Carbohydrates: 5 g / Protein: 12 g / Sodium: 358 mg / Fat: 29 g (Saturated Fat: 8 g) / Potassium: 187 mg.

SALAD NIÇOISE

Makes 8 Servings

8	tiny new potatoes (about ¾ pound)
2½	cups green beans, cooked to crisp-tender and drained (1 pound fresh)
1	small red onion, sliced
½	cup Niçoise olives *or* ripe olives
¼	cup snipped Italian parsley *or* regular parsley
½	teaspoon salt
½	teaspoon pepper
¼	cup red wine vinegar
1	tablespoon Dijon-style mustard
1	teaspoon sugar
¼	teaspoon salt
¼	teaspoon pepper
1	tablespoon finely snipped parsley *or* chives
½	cup olive oil
8	ripe Italian plum tomatoes, quartered
4	hard-cooked eggs, halved *or* sliced
1	12- or 13-ounce can water-packed tuna, drained

❖   ❖   ❖

Donna DeBoer says that she often makes Salad Niçoise for her family to take on their boat as delicious fare for hot summer nights.

Donna DeBoer
International Cookbook
Pamoja International Cultural Exchange, Inc.
Helena
NEW YORK

1 Cook the potatoes in salted boiling water about 10 minutes or until just tender. Drain. Cut the potatoes into quarters and place in a large bowl.

2 Stir in the green beans, onion, olives, parsley, the ½ teaspoon salt and the ½ teaspoon pepper.

3 To make the vinaigrette: In a small bowl, whisk together the vinegar, mustard, sugar, the ¼ teaspoon salt, the ¼ teaspoon pepper and the parsley or chives. Gradually whisk in the olive oil. Continue whisking until the mixture thickens slightly.

4 Pour about *half* of the vinaigrette over the vegetable mixture and toss gently.

5 Transfer the vegetable mixture to a large serving platter. Arrange the tomatoes and eggs around the edge of the platter. Flake the tuna and spoon it on top of the vegetable mixture. Drizzle the entire salad with the remaining vinaigrette. Serve immediately.

TIPS FROM OUR KITCHEN

Niçoise olives are dark brown, tiny, brine-cured and packed in olive oil.

Salad Niçoise is traditionally served at room temperature, although you can chill it if you prefer. Of course, be sure to refrigerate any leftovers.

To prepare the fresh green beans: Wash and remove the ends and strings. Cook, covered, in a small amount of boiling water for 20 to 25 minutes.

You can substitute two 9-ounce packages of frozen cut green beans for the fresh beans in the recipe. Cook them according to the package directions.

Hard-cooked eggs sometimes have a harmless, but unattractive greenish ring around the yolk or are difficult to peel. To minimize these possibilities, place the eggs in a single layer in a saucepan. Add cold water to a level 1 inch above the eggs. Bring to a boil over high heat. Reduce the heat so that the water is just below simmering. Cover and cook for 15 minutes. Drain the eggs immediately and cool them in an ice-water bath.

Nutrition Analysis (*Per Serving*): Calories: 301 / Cholesterol: 124 mg / Carbohydrates: 18 g / Protein: 17 g / Sodium: 498 mg / Fat: 19 g (Saturated Fat: 3 g) / Potassium: 551 mg.

SALAD NIÇOISE

CONFETTI RICE SALAD

CONFETTI RICE SALAD

Makes 6 Servings

⅔	cup long grain rice
¼	teaspoon salt
2	tablespoons snipped parsley
1 to 2	tablespoons snipped fresh dill
½	teaspoon finely shredded lemon peel
2	tablespoons lemon juice
2	tablespoons water
2	tablespoons olive oil
1	teaspoon Dijon-style mustard
⅛	teaspoon pepper
1	cup finely chopped yellow summer squash
1	cup small broccoli flowerets
3	radishes, thinly sliced
1	green onion, thinly sliced

◆   ◆   ◆

While visiting the Bahamas years ago, Gloria Pattison tried to prepare the original version of this dish but was unable to find several ingredients. To solve the problem, she substituted yellow squash and radishes—along with a few other ingredients—and the result was this tasty version of Confetti Rice Salad.

Gloria Pattison
A Dunker Cookbook
The North County Church
of the Brethren
San Marcos
CALIFORNIA

1 In a small saucepan, combine 1½ cups *water*, the rice and salt. Bring to a boil; reduce heat to low. Cover and cook for 20 minutes.

2 Transfer the cooked rice to a sieve. Rinse the rice under cold water. Drain and set aside.

3 In a large bowl, stir together the parsley, dill, lemon peel, lemon juice, the 2 tablespoons water, the olive oil, Dijon-style mustard and pepper.

4 Add the rice, yellow summer squash, broccoli, radishes and green onion. Toss until the mixture is well coated. Cover and chill for 4 to 24 hours, stirring occasionally.

 TIPS FROM OUR KITCHEN

For a change, substitute halved cherry tomatoes or chopped red sweet pepper for the radishes. Or, replace part of the yellow summer squash with chopped yellow sweet peppers.

If fresh dill isn't available, you can use 1 to 2 teaspoons dried dillweed.

To make fun and attractive individual serving bowls, wash and remove the stems and seeds from 3 large or 6 small green, red or yellow sweet peppers. Cut the larger peppers in half lengthwise. Spoon in the salad.

If desired, blanch the broccoli before adding it to the salad. Blanching makes the broccoli more tender and brings out the bright green color.

To get flowerets, trim the leaves from the broccoli and wash it under cold, running water. Cut off just the flowerets with a sharp knife. Reserve the stalks to use later in soups and casseroles.

Nutrition Analysis (*Per Serving*): Calories: 129 / Cholesterol: 0 mg / Carbohydrates: 19 g / Protein: 3 g / Sodium: 121 mg / Fat: 5 g (Saturated Fat: 1 g) / Potassium: 160 mg.

SPINACH SALAD DUO

Makes 6 to 8 Servings
Salad:
1   pound fresh spinach, rinsed and well dried (12 cups)
2   small apples, finely chopped
½   cup crumbled blue cheese
½   cup broken walnuts
Dressing:
1   cup mayonnaise *or* salad dressing
½   cup dairy sour cream
¼   cup crumbled blue cheese
¼   teaspoon salt
⅛   teaspoon coarsely ground pepper
6   slices bacon, crisply cooked and crumbled

♦   ♦   ♦

Using text, recipes, drawings and photos, From a Lighthouse Window succeeds in presenting a satisfying glimpse into Maryland's Eastern Shore "where crab is king and the oyster has a place in history." The bounty of the Chesapeake waters and fertile farmlands have contributed to a distinct culinary legacy, which survives today for all to enjoy.

From a Lighthouse Window
Chesapeake Bay Maritime Museum
St. Michaels
MARYLAND

1 To make the salad: Remove the tough stems from the spinach and discard. Tear the spinach into bite-size pieces.

2 In a very large bowl, toss together the spinach, apples, the ½ cup blue cheese and the walnuts. Cover and refrigerate until ready to serve.

3 To make the dressing: In a small bowl, stir together the mayonnaise or salad dressing, sour cream, the ¼ cup blue cheese, the salt and pepper. Cover and refrigerate until ready to serve.

4 Just before serving, pour the dressing over the spinach mixture. Gently toss. Sprinkle with the bacon and serve immediately.

TIPS FROM OUR KITCHEN

Before you begin, make sure your salad bowl will hold at least 14 cups of salad mixture.

For a lighter version of the dressing, substitute ¼ cup *milk* and 1 tablespoon *honey* for the mayonnaise.

Don't add the dressing to the salad until just before serving. If you do, the spinach will become limp and the dressing will get watery.

If time is short, look for precleaned spinach. Otherwise, you can wash it thoroughly the day before you need to make the salad. To wash, rinse the spinach thoroughly in cold water to remove all of the sand from the crinkly leaves. Pat dry and store in a paper towel-lined plastic bag.

Toasting the walnuts will help to keep them crisp in the salad. To toast: Place the nuts in a small skillet and cook over medium heat for 5 to 7 minutes or until the walnuts are golden, stirring often. Let the walnuts cool before adding them to the salad.

The term *blue cheese* includes several varieties of blue-veined, semisoft cheeses. Gorgonzola is softer, creamier and less pungent than most blue cheeses. Roquefort is made from whole sheep's milk and is produced only within the city of Roquefort, France. Stilton is made only in England.

Nutrition Analysis (*Per Serving*): Calories: 488 / Cholesterol: 46 mg / Carbohydrates: 11 g / Protein: 10 g / Sodium: 674 mg / Fat: 47 g (Saturated Fat: 11 g) / Potassium: 611 mg.

SPINACH SALAD DUO

POPPY SEED SALAD

POPPY SEED SALAD

Makes 10 to 12 Servings

- 4 cups torn iceberg lettuce
- 4 cups torn spinach
- 4 cups shredded red cabbage
- 1 11-ounce can mandarin orange sections, drained
- 12 to 15 strawberries, quartered (1½ cups)
- ½ red onion, sliced and separated into rings (½ cup)

Dressing:
- ¾ cup cider vinegar
- ⅔ cup honey
- 1 medium onion, cut up
- 3 tablespoons prepared mustard
- 3 tablespoons poppy seed

◆　　◆　　◆

Tricia Haney, Cookbook Chairperson for The Fort Leavenworth Recollection, said that because military life is so transient, friends and family often have to adapt their recipes to use local ingredients. The cookbook is filled with a variety of dishes from Fort Leavenworth residents.

Tami Lamar
The Fort Leavenworth Recollection
The Fort Leavenworth Officers and Civilians Wives' Club
Fort Leavenworth
KANSAS

1 In a large salad bowl, toss together the iceberg lettuce, spinach, red cabbage, mandarin orange sections, strawberries and red onion slices. Cover and refrigerate the salad until serving time.

2 To make the dressing: In a blender container or food processor bowl, combine the cider vinegar, honey, onion, mustard, ½ teaspoon *salt* and a dash of *white* or *black pepper.* Cover and blend or process until nearly smooth. Stir in the poppy seed. Pour the dressing into a bowl or large jar, cover and refrigerate until serving time.

3 To serve, add *half* of the dressing to the salad. Toss to coat the salad ingredients well with the dressing. Store the remaining dressing in the refrigerator for use another time.

 TIPS FROM OUR KITCHEN

For this recipe, you will need about ⅔ of a 1-pound head of cabbage. You can shred the red cabbage by pushing wedges through the feed tube of a food processor or by coarsely chopping thin slices.

To quarter strawberries: Cut the strawberries lengthwise in half, then make another cut perpendicular to the first cut.

Use the remaining dressing with a spinach salad or drizzle the dressing over fresh or canned fruit.

Nutrition Analysis (*Per Serving*): Calories: 85 / Cholesterol: 0 mg / Carbohydrates: 20 g / Protein: 2 g / Sodium: 112 mg / Fat: 1 g (Saturated Fat: 0 g) / Potassium: 330 mg.

recipe index